MY SEXUAL AWAKENING AT 70

∽and what led me here∽

To Hanna,
Enjoy!
Lynn Rosenberg

A MEMOIR

LYNN BROWN ROSENBERG

MY SEXUAL AWAKENING AT 70

~and what led me here~

A MEMOIR

Direct inquiries to: www.LynnBrownRosenberg.com

Edited by EbookEditingServices.com
Cover Design by Digital Donna
Formatted by IRONHORSE Formatting

Printed in the United States of America.

ISBN-13: 978-0-578-15029-1

DEDICATION

To B.

In Loving Memory

INTRODUCTION

I was determined to take back ownership of the right to a healthy, satisfying sex life. Even if it took me to age seventy to do it!

I had always been in search of the truth about life, love, and sex, but it remained out of my grasp. Through this memoir, I have uncovered it under layers of misinformation, manipulation, and sometimes even lies.

In joining a sex chat website, where I engaged in sexually graphic chats with men, I realized that I was sexually repressed. My initial goal was to expand my sexual horizons, but it became so much more. Once the floodgates opened sexually, my psychological restraints fell away, also. The influences that had led me to protect myself by shutting down emotionally faded, and freedom emerged.

As I evolved, I began to write erotica and these stories are interspersed throughout this book. They were another way to explore my sensuality and became integral to my growth. I am pleased to share them with you.

Reader Caution: This book contains frank, and sometimes raw, sexual discussion and descriptions. If you are easily offended, this may not be the book for you. Please do not leave this book where it might be viewed by minors.

~

I hope that you gain courage and benefit from what I have done and find your own path to freedom and truth, whatever that may be, and wherever that may lead you.

Starter Sex - 2012

I wanted mad, passionate, down-and-dirty sex.

∽

The first person to contact me was Dave. According to his photo, Dave was a very attractive young man. Thirty-three years young, in fact. I was sixty-nine. I immediately discounted him because of our huge age difference, yet I made no move to leave the site.

"Would you like to chat?" he wrote.

"Don't you want someone closer to your age?" I wrote back, stalling for time, both afraid and excited about where this was heading.

"I've tried. They're mostly scams."

"What do you mean?"

"Women who want money."

The time for a decision was near. What was I going to do next, if anything?

"Are you horny?" he wrote.

I was aching with desire. I looked at his picture again. He had a day-old scruff, full lips, and a sexy smile. I was hesitant, but I knew I had to do it.

"Yes," I answered.

"What do you like?"

"Naughty chat," I wrote.

"Would you want to meet in person sometime?"

"Maybe," I answered, never ever intending to meet him or anyone else from this site.

I pulled out my notes from my favorite porn video to see if I could get Dave under my spell the way the porn actress had done with her male counterpart.

"What are you wearing?" Dave wrote.

"See-through nightie." I was actually wearing jeans and a T-shirt, but my goal was to arouse him.

"I want to give you a soft and sensual kiss."

My bedroom was starting to feel warm. "Are you stroking yourself?" I asked a perfect stranger.

"Yes," Dave answered.

"Are you hard?" I wrote. My face felt hot. My body felt hotter. Referring to my notes, I then wrote, "Would you like me to take the tip of your cock inside my mouth and suck on it?"

"Yeah, baby," he answered.

I continued to read from my notes, without which I

would have been lost. My heart was racing. I was embarrassed! Excited! Writing word for word, question after question what the woman in the video said. I was breaking with all propriety, everything I had learned from my parents about how to be a nice Jewish girl.

A short time later, Dave had what he described as a powerful orgasm, and he thanked me repeatedly. Should I be thanked for such a thing?

When we finished, I masturbated to thoughts of Dave and our dialogue.

Later that night, I reflected on what had happened. What on earth had I done? Should I have done it? *I can stop now*, I told myself. *I just won't go back online.* Regardless of the questions racing through my mind, I was aware of one thing: I had enjoyed myself! Because of that, I knew I had to push the boundaries. I had to see where this would take me.

There was no denying it; this was a new beginning.

My Mother Was a Virgin – 1940
or
The Road to Repression

I read somewhere that we are born sexual human beings. But there is always an exception to the rule, isn't there?

Three months after my parents met in Chicago, they had a blink-and-it's-over wedding, comprised of family, a few friends, and some inexpensive champagne. My mother was nineteen and a virgin when she married my father. Her virginity was totally in keeping with the mores of the day. She took great pride in this, and didn't allow herself to fall sway to my father's seductive charms when they were dating, like a few of her girlfriends had done with their men. I came to understand that my father tried his best to persuade her, and had she given in to him, he never would have married her. It was a test, and my mother dazzled him with her resistance. While holding off sex for three months wasn't a long time, my father, I was told, was very persistent!

They honeymooned in Florida to check out the dream of living there, but my mother had reservations. They returned to Chicago, and their life together as Muriel and Phil Brown began. My father hated Chicago winters and he'd remind my mother that Florida had great weather. But it also had bugs. Insects the size of rodents. Or perhaps they were rodents. That's how my mother described them to me. The subject of moving to Florida stalled when my mother became pregnant with me. They stayed put until I was born, which took place at dawn on November 16, 1942. A few months later they headed west, arriving in Los Angeles to make a new life. Great weather. No bugs.

Nana's Affair – 1936

Just because we moved to California didn't mean everything was left behind in Chicago.

Shortly after settling into our small, one-bedroom apartment in Hollywood, my dad started his upholstery business. He arranged for my grandparents on both sides to come out to Los Angeles, except for my mother's father, Louis, who had died right before I was born. In the Jewish religion, it's traditional to name your child after a deceased relative, using their first initial or their name. That's how I came to be named Lynn. Unless you counted holiday dinners, it would be the last religious experience my family ever had.

But getting back to remembrances of things past, my mother often spoke of her admiration for her father. He'd been an attorney until, yet early in his career, he was diagnosed with both multiple sclerosis and diabetes, and was left an invalid a short time later. She said at one time she had desired to be an attorney like him.

My grandmother, Nana, on the other hand, had a whole different set of feelings. She didn't take well to caregiving, and even less to sacrifice, escaping for brief periods of time to have an affair with a married man. My mother, who had so much respect for her father, lost it for her mother.

On the rare occasion (these things were not discussed), when a barb was tossed in Nana's direction about the affair, my grandmother would defend her behavior vehemently as if it were the only course of action possible in such a situation. She also blushed and giggled.

Nana had, when it came to this subject, a lightness of spirit. I think there's a very good chance she would have left my grandfather (circumstances be damned!) if her lover had asked that of her. But given that he already had a wife to whom he was evidently attached, the opportunity never presented itself.

I wondered if my grandfather's death wasn't a greater loss to my mother than she acknowledged, and her mother's infidelity a harbinger of things to come with regard to her attitude toward sex. Maybe her ironclad resistance to my father's advances before marriage evolved more from disgust with my grandmother's behavior, rather than a fearsome battle within herself to stay pure.

Nana never remarried.

~

My other grandmother *should* have had an affair. If
so, she might never have had a stroke. My father's mother,
Celia, had been beautiful in her youth. But she had
disappointed herself and her parents by marrying a house
painter, a sweet but simple man. Soon she lost her looks,
became ill, and focused her world on her only son. She had
always doted on him, teaching him how to sew at an early
age which prepared him for his future as an upholsterer.
But now it was more intense. Celia was always thanking
God to be near "her Philly", as she called him. Still, while
another mother might have found peace being reunited with
her son whenever time allowed them to get together, that
wasn't enough for my grandma. She might be thanking
God, but she was a complex and clever woman. She loved
her Philly, all right, but impromptu visits by my father
weren't enough. There was always an aftertaste following
a visit with her. A sentence unfinished. Something else on
her mind. Jealous of my mother, Grandma would accuse
my father of not loving her because of the attention he paid
to my mother. So my father did what he thought would
appease both Grandma and my mother, who was now
feeling neglected by Grandma's demands. He moved
Grandma and Grandpa right down the hall from our
apartment!

It didn't work well, but it didn't fail either. By having
them so close it minimized travel time back and forth to
visit, and my father could semi-satisfy both Grandma and
my mother. In truth, neither one was happy, but at least
there were no shouting matches and nobody threatened to

leave anybody.

In retrospect, I believe my mother learned some of her manipulation skills from my grandma. After all, she had the opportunity to see firsthand how well these skills paid off. Until the day my grandma died, my mother and their marriage came second with my father. Grandma Brown ate manipulator pie for breakfast, lunch, and dinner. My mother was no match for the first woman to possess and control my father's heart.

My Journey Begins - Summer 2011

A mere six months before engaging in "starter sex" with Dave, I had been a different person. I'd been a widow for fifteen years with only a handful of dates that entire time. I still had hopes of finding another soul mate. In my first few years of being on my own, I could not, and would not, consider a new relationship. I was too raw from Jerry's death. Six years of dreading the next blood test, MRI, or phone call had taken its toll. And in between those there'd been a new drug, new hope, or new procedure that could possibly save or prolong his life.

~

But many years had passed and I was interested again, not just in a relationship but in a highly erotic connection, something that had been missing from my marriage. Before our fifteen-year marriage, I was fortunate to have had a few great lovers. I knew the difference. There were times I felt Jerry could have been more curious about what made me tick sexually. I tried to communicate what pleased me but he wasn't able to interpret my wishes. Still, I have come to realize that my part measured at least half, if not more, on the blame meter. It never occurred to me to experiment with Jerry, either using sex toys or porn, or even different places or ways to have sex. The idea that sex could be playful or fun wasn't something that entered my mind. Without knowing it, I was trapped sexually. For Jerry's part, I will never know if he felt that way too because, unbelievably, we never discussed it.

While I'd been told by my girlfriends I looked "good for my age" (the worst kind of compliment there is), I wasn't meeting anyone. I knew I was reasonably attractive—short dark hair, hazel eyes, shapely body, good height at 5'5", and a youthful face. It had been enough of a challenge to meet the right man when I was in my twenties and thirties; in my sixties, it seemed almost impossible.

Due to an unsuccessful business venture I was forced to sell my condominium in Marina del Rey, California. I moved in with a roommate, but she was not the type of woman you'd bring a boyfriend back home to. She could be moody, unpredictable, and territorial about her condo. If I wanted sex, I'd have to move out.

Leaving meant moving out of the posh Marina for a more economically viable living situation. I searched but I wasn't coming up with any options. I put myself on a couple of lists for more affordable housing, but I was told it could take a long time. Until then, I would have to remain where I was.

How long would I have to wait before I could invite a new lover into my bed? How long would I have to wait before my new life could start?

Lisa - 2011

The few dates I had after Jerry died were chaste. What that means is that I'd been in a fifteen-year drought. Did anyone go for fifteen years without sex? After my mother passed away, my father told me he had not had sex in five years. After I regained enough composure to think clearly, I recall feeling stunned that anyone could manage that long without sex, never thinking that I might one day beat his record by ten years! I had no interest in his reason for abstinence, but I think my own unfortunate happenstance was due to a medication I was taking that knocked out my sex drive.

Somewhere along the line, I requested and received a new prescription from my physician and traded in my Prozac for Prestiq and Abilify. I also met a man to whom I was very attracted. He was intelligent, funny, and dynamic. He was also married. Suddenly, because of the chemistry between us and my change in meds, my sexual urges came alive. I wanted this man. But not only was he married, he was happily married and had never cheated on his wife. Realistically, a coupling was not going to happen.

Around this same time, I met a neighbor named Lisa. Lisa would tell lively stories of her dating life. She had joined Match.com and had met a man she liked, but he had a son and often cancelled on Lisa at the last minute to do something with him. Having become frustrated and dissatisfied, she dropped the man and Match.com.

Several months later Lisa decided to have professional pictures taken. She was going to join another dating site. Her picture was a knockout. Lisa was fifty-three but she looked forty-three. She posted the photo on JDate.com, the Jewish dating site. If her date from Match.com had been frustrating, the stories she would tell me now were about guy after guy who didn't look anything like his picture, was a disappointment in the way he behaved, and was cheap or didn't have a job. Not meeting anyone she liked on JDate, she decided to join the free site OkCupid.com where a surge of younger men contacted her. Curious, she decided to date a few of them, but they posed a different set of problems. Although she was flattered to receive so much attention from men decades her junior, because of the age difference these relationships would go nowhere.

Despite her tribulations, Lisa suggested I join too. Misery loves company I guess. Years before I had given those same sites a try with no luck, so I was not eager to get back into the fray. But the idea of having a professional picture taken awakened new hope in me. So I joined also.

I did meet a nice man, Alan, who treated me well. We went out for lunch once, then to dinner and a movie the next time. I wanted to find Alan attractive but I just didn't. He had a bad habit of eating with his mouth open, and when he spoke, food shot across the table in my direction. This completely turned me off.

Nothing much happened on the website after that. But something did happen with housing. An apartment opened up in Long Beach, about thirty minutes from the Marina. It was bright and like new. I saw potential for a new beginning. And the best part? I would have privacy!

Larry - 2011

Lisa and I began spending more time together as we had dating in common. Well, I wasn't dating, but I was interested in dating, and that was enough for us to bond. And between listening to her experiences, and learning of a new website that didn't charge anything to join, I felt pretty sure meeting someone was right around the corner.

The website suggested that in order to increase your chances of meeting someone you should make the first move, even if you were the woman. I followed this advice. I did find a man I was interested in and sent him a message. Larry responded to my inquiry immediately and said we should meet. On his profile, he stated that he was a movie producer. Since I had written several screenplays I liked the fact that he was in show business. I was also attracted to his gray hair which was slicked back into a ponytail (did I say I liked a ponytail?), and his full mouth. We met for afternoon drinks at El Torito, a popular Mexican restaurant, the Friday after Thanksgiving. I was as drawn to Larry in person as I had been to his picture on the website. Things were looking up.

He guided me to the bar and we sat down. The room was dimly lit, which made everyone look better than they ordinarily would. I know I felt more attractive. We ordered margaritas. It was happy hour so for a little extra we could have Grand Marnier in them. He motioned "yes" to the bartender. A television above the bar was tuned to some sort of ball game. I didn't pay any attention to it but Larry did. I wasn't a sports fan so I had no idea what game was being played or anything about the teams. Larry didn't talk much, but started muttering something about losing $8,000 because his cell phone had run out of juice. I didn't know what he was talking about, but he kept repeating it. Apparently, he wasn't able to place a bet on the game being broadcast because his cell phone went dead on the way over to meet me.

"I'm pissed," he said repeatedly.

Meanwhile, I was thinking, *What in the world am I doing with this guy?*

"Do you understand what just happened?" he asked.

"You're a bookie!" I answered.

"I shouldn't have told you."

At that point I didn't know whether he should or shouldn't have told me. I just knew I felt like I was in a different zone, not knowing how to respond to this guy or whether I should leave. And then the strangest thing happened: he kissed me.

This was no ordinary kiss. It was probably the most sensual, out-of-this-world kiss I have ever had in my life. Afterward, I took a sip of my drink and turned back in his direction in hopes he would repeat it, knowing it could never be as good as the first time.

He kissed me again, and it was as good as the first one if not better. I was completely transfixed. Then he leaned in and kissed my shoulder. I was high, I was low, and my head was spinning. Now what? We had a second round of drinks and something to eat. He wanted to order me a third drink and come home with me, but I said no to both. At the bar, in front of God and everybody, he tried to lower my hand to his crotch. I resisted. Kissing was one thing, this was another.

When the bar finally closed down, we extracted ourselves and left. Once outside, he asked me where he stood on a ratio of one-to-ten. I said about a six or seven. I didn't know if that was true or not. He was a zero for being a bookie, but a ten for kissing. So that averaged out I guessed, to a seven. He asked if I was going to see him again.

"I don't know," I said.

"C'mon, you can tell me," he replied.

"I don't know," I repeated. "I have to think about it. If we ever do see each other again, would you please wear that same aftershave?" I wanted to inhale it all night. It had a clean scent with a hint of musk. It was sensual, sexy, him.

He didn't try to kiss me again, much to my

disappointment, and though I thought he would walk me to my car, he didn't do that either.

I lived just a few blocks from the restaurant, and it wasn't long before I realized Larry was in the next lane to me. My first thought was, *Oh my God, he's following me!* I actually felt fear. Then it occurred to me he must have lost his way because the freeway was behind us. I lowered my window and told him so, and a minute later he was gone.

The next day I called Lisa. I told her about the date and the kiss, and conferred with her as to whether I should see him again.

She said, "Why not? As long as you don't get serious about him."

I was really surprised. That wasn't the answer I expected. Then I called my girlfriend Jeanette and asked her the same question, certain she would tell me under no circumstances should I see a bookie again, but she repeated what Lisa had said. Suddenly, the veil lifted. I thought, *Wow, I could actually have more of those kisses.*

Larry had asked me to call him instead of the other way around. I felt awkward, but I did what he wanted. He said he was really surprised to hear from me, that he hadn't thought I would call. After we exchanged niceties, I felt compelled to say something about his aggressive behavior.

"I need to tell you I thought you were too pushy."

"I didn't mean to be," he said. "I'm just at the age where I believe in doing what I want to do."

I thought he would make another date with me but he

didn't. I was left feeling deflated. Over the course of the next several days, I made up my mind that I wanted to have sex with him. Too much frustration had built up over the last year with my married friend and now being exposed to Larry's kisses, combined with the shocking approval of my friends, brought me to the point of no return. I had to sleep with this man.

But suddenly, Larry was hard to pin down. He made a tentative date with me, then wasn't available when I called him. Yes, I called him. He had asked me to. I didn't know what was with him and telephoning me, but I could see it wasn't going to happen. A week passed …a long week …until we finally made firm plans to meet again.

Larry - Round 2

We met at El Torito again. We went to the bar, sat on the same barstools, and ordered the same margaritas. Only this time Larry was more verbal, talking about his family, his childhood, his children, his children's significant others.

After an hour or more had passed, I was feeling somewhat impatient, and asked, "Aren't you going to kiss me?"

And finally, he did. But it wasn't the same as those thrilling kisses the time before. Still, I wasn't giving up. I was determined to take him home with me.

We entered my apartment, and I went to the bathroom to freshen up. I removed my clothes and put on a *pareo*, leaving my panties on. I figured he should be able to take off something.

One important fact ... I didn't have a bed yet. I had ordered one but it wasn't scheduled to be delivered for two more weeks. I hadn't had a bed for the last year and a half.

At my old roommate's condo I had wanted the feel of an office rather than a bedroom, so I gave up my bed and slept on my sofa. Somehow I felt better about myself that way. In my mind, I was being productive. A bed symbolized just a bedroom to me.

I informed Larry we'd have to use the sofa, but he didn't seem to mind.

We began making love. We tried to get comfortable, but couldn't. Fumbling for balance, we moved to the floor. It was awkward for both of us, but we were determined.

Sex was fantastic. I had forgotten how truly wonderful it was, how great it felt to have a man inside me. All the words in the dictionary rolled into one could not adequately describe the sensation. Larry was well-endowed, which made it all the more visually and physically exciting for me. As we were having sex I looked in his eyes. They were half-closed and glazed over as if he were in another world. Earlier, he had let me know he hadn't had sex in a long time either. I knew it couldn't possibly be as long as me. In fact, in the last day or two I had idly wondered if the length of time I had gone without sex could have set some sort of record. Anyway, the two of us definitely enjoyed ourselves. And then, a few minutes later he gave me all he had, which I received willingly, wantonly.

It was odd afterward though. Not really knowing each other at all, we had nothing much to say. The fact that I didn't have a bed didn't make it conducive to cuddling or having any kind of intimate talk, though even if there had been a bed I'm not sure we would have engaged in much conversation. What would we have talked about? He got dressed, said he had to get up early the next day, and asked if I wanted to do this again sometime.

I said, "Yes."

He said, again, "Call me."

I didn't. After sex, I felt it was his place to call me. But he didn't.

Larry had given me his business card and made me an offer: if I knew, or could find, someone who'd like to invest in a movie, he would pay me a finder's fee. Despite my economically challenging circumstances, I didn't care about the finder's fee, but I did want another chance at sex with him. I could have just called him, as he suggested, but decided my chances would be better if I actually did find someone who might invest. I phoned a friend who had a friend who wanted to see the script.

In the meantime, my bed was delivered. I hoped Larry would christen it.

I called Larry and left him a message that I might have an investor. He phoned me right back. It turned out that his company's policy was such that no scripts would be sent out to potential investors, so that killed that. However, I got the chance to tell him I now had a bed and that I thought we'd be much more comfortable if we had another go at it.

He said he'd really enjoyed our time together but, "You live so far."

He lived in Hollywood. It was about ninety minutes to Long Beach on a good day. I understood his objection, but

I knew if he really wanted to be with me he would have made it work. I never saw Larry again.

The Beginning of Crazy – 1946

An early memory creeps into my consciousness. I was four years old. I try hard to push the image out of my mind, but the more I do the more it holds fast. I tell myself this was irrelevant to my sexual development, but I know this isn't true. This is where the slow strangling of my thoughts and feelings first began.

It was just before dawn. I stood rigid in the hallway. I sensed something awful was about to happen. My mother picked up the phone and dialed. I knew she was angry. I had just wet my bed. She told me I shouldn't be wetting the bed at four years old.

"Is this the bad girls' school?" she asked, speaking into the phone.

For a moment all was silent.

"My daughter has been a bad girl. Would you come over and pick her up?"

"Please don't send me away, Mommy!" I screamed. I begged. I cried.

She held the phone up to her ear for what felt like a very long time and then finally hung up.

~

Not long after, I turned five. My mother had a celebration for me. My parents, grandparents, and Nana sang the happy birthday song. Cake and coffee, and presents were served. My mother was smiling, laughing even, like nothing had ever happened. I had no siblings or friends; there were no other children present. I opened up a gift and pulled out two dolls, a bride and groom. Marriage. The goal of every young girl in the late 1940s.

"Hold them up, Lynn," my father said, as he raised the camera to his face. "Now, smile."

~

The constant inconsistency, on a daily basis, of abuse one minute and gifts the next, would cost me my ability to function normally. Who my parents were and how they treated me led me to hide who I truly was. Repression resulted. The intimidation, insults, and denial of my existence as an individual with my own mind and feelings bled into every area of my life.

My Mother – Continued

My mother believed in looking "smart" for her man.
Over the years she varied her appearance to keep my father
interested. Her natural hair color was brunette, and she
would occasionally return to it, but she also tried blond,
red, and strawberry blond. Leaning toward glamour, she
finally settled on blond. My mother never went without
makeup. How you looked and how you behaved in front of
others was as precious to her as if they were
commandments carved in stone: "Thou shalt always look
attractive," and "Thou shalt always behave properly."

My mother aspired to perfection. Never was a hair out
of place. She never even broke into a sweat as far as I could
tell.

And though she may have been inexperienced when
she married my father, she was determined to learn and
grow. She began to follow fashion, and her impeccable
taste would prove helpful to her later on. Her clothes were

refined yet feminine and earned the admiration of all her friends.

My mother taught herself to become an outstanding cook, and to knit and sew ably. She was a woman who could do anything she set her mind to. Her friends admired those qualities, as did I. But her friends never saw the woman behind closed doors, the woman who never touched or hugged her daughter, and never told her she loved her.

Sometimes I'd see a mother giving her child a warm embrace and feel a surge of envy. Other times I'd notice the soft touch of a mother's hand on her child's cheek and I'd look on, wondering what that must feel like. My father tried to explain it away by telling me she just wasn't affectionate but that she loved me. But you know whether you're loved or not. If you're told it secondhand, it doesn't hold much value. Not to me, anyway.

I never felt loved by my mother no matter how often my father would repeat the well-worn phrase, "She just isn't an affectionate woman but she loves you."

It was true she wasn't affectionate with anyone, even my father, but that didn't make it any easier for me.

~

There was always the threat that my mother's life would be cut short. She had diabetes and her health was part of nearly every conversation as far back as I can remember. If she made it through one catastrophe, another was sure to follow. At what age would I be when the end came and I'd be without a mother? That question loomed over me from the time I was a young child.

In her late forties, my mother's eyesight was starting to deteriorate which was a side effect of Type 1 diabetes. She and my father faced the likelihood that one day she would go blind. They sought the help of the Jules Styne Institute at the University of California, Los Angeles, but they couldn't seem to help her. And just because one problem was addressed, that didn't mean there weren't others that cropped up. Because of the diabetes, there was always the threat that one day her kidneys might fail, or that she could lose a limb from poor circulation and gangrene setting in.

Besides cooking and baking rich desserts, my mother also enjoyed her cocktails, which was typical of that era; however, these were potentially fatal to a diabetic. Although she was never overweight, she did not watch her sugar. And probably the worst of all for a diabetic, she smoked and refused to give it up. Smoking was very bad for her circulation, which was vital to her good health. But she didn't care. She defied the doctors.

She'd say, "When it's my time to go, I'll go."

It was always painful for me to hear her talk like that. The doctors did what they could but ultimately, if my mother wanted to self-destruct, there was nothing they could do to prevent it. My mother's opinion of the doctors changed with the wind, however. When it supported a belief of hers she took the advice; when it didn't, she ignored it.

And while she debated how much credence, if any, to give the doctors' warnings, I don't think she ever considered what her devil-may-care attitude toward her health did to my father and me: the constant anxiety, the expense (being diabetic at that time meant she couldn't be insured), and having to put our lives on hold while she, with great drama, lived hers.

Shane - 2012

One day Lisa called and told me about another free dating website, so both of us went on it. It took me many months to forget about Larry. I didn't flip from one person to the next easily. No one roused my interest on the dating sites, until finally I found another man whose picture I liked. Shane sounded more substantial than Larry in every way. I wrote him and like Larry, he wrote back right away, wanting to meet me. I told him if he gave me his phone number I would call him. I had a blocked number so I felt safer calling him rather than giving out my number. He ignored my suggestion and emailed me back that he would be happy to drive from Trabuco Canyon, about an hour away, to meet me. I became alarmed. Why didn't this guy want to talk to me on the phone? And what was his rush?

A few weeks passed without contact. I had hoped he would write and offer to have a phone conversation, but he didn't. And I was reticent to meet with someone whose voice I had not heard.

It is easy to become insecure on a dating site. It's often difficult to know if the tone of your message was received in the light you intended, and there is always that nagging doubt as to how much of the information you receive is really true. I emailed Shane again, asking him if by not agreeing to meet him without a phone conversation, I had put him off? He responded "Absolutely not," and that when he returned from Kauai two weeks hence on May 18, he would contact me. Somewhere around that time, I clicked on his profile again and reread it. I saw something I hadn't seen before. He had wonderful qualities: he liked five-star hotels, enjoyed travel, plays, and movies, and then came the last item. Under interests, one of the last items was *endless foreplay.* If I'd been interested in Shane before, I was impassioned now and determined to have an erotic experience with him.

After May 18 I noticed he had returned because I saw that he was online. But I didn't want to be pushy. So I waited. Three days passed. I wanted to write him badly, but I held back. On the afternoon of the fourth day, his profile was *gone.* Nowhere to be found. He had signed himself off the site. And I will never, ever know why. I didn't know if he was married, and if he was, whether his wife found out. I didn't know if he'd met someone in that short period of time. I didn't know. And that was the worst outcome of all.

Orgasms - 2011

Without meeting anyone, I was becoming increasingly more sexually frustrated. Orgasms had never come easily to me but I hadn't thought of ever mentioning it to a doctor or therapist to see whether there was something available to help me. Finally, I did. After listening to me carefully, my urologist, a woman, gave me her prescription: a vibrator and some porn. Wow!

Thirty years before, a married cousin had mentioned she sometimes used a vibrator and suggested it for me.

"Interesting," I said, while silently scoffing at the idea.

I couldn't imagine myself stooping that low. Until that moment I hadn't had a high regard for porn frankly, labeling it in my head as disgusting. And I thought the people who watched it were either deviant, desperate, or both. Now, suddenly, those judgments flew out the window. Now, not only was I not having sex, I wasn't having orgasms. I was ready to stoop.

I drove to a specialty shop in West Hollywood. I figured I would just rush right in, buy something, and rush right out before anyone I knew, God forbid, might see me. Nice Jewish girls didn't hang out at porn shops. As I drove there I was filled with anxiety.

I entered the doors to The Pleasure Chest (the name alone gave me heart palpitations) and was quite surprised. The products were laid out very nicely. The salesgirl was helpful and not at all judgmental. I almost felt comfortable.

There were so many items to choose from! But ultimately I decided on Budding Bliss, a clitoral stimulator and g-spot vibrator all in one. I also bought a porn DVD titled *Wicked Games*. I chose that one because...why not? If I was going to stoop, why not stoop all the way?

Much to my surprise, I began having orgasms. It became my new hobby. Orgasm in the afternoon (Lisa called it "afternoon delight") and orgasm in the evening. This went on for, incredibly, two weeks. And suddenly the orgasms stopped. I seemed to need greater or different stimuli to be able to climax.

I mentioned the problem to my therapist and said that I couldn't be spending money on porn DVDs endlessly. He told me there was free internet porn. My horizons were expanding.

I looked for free porn on the internet and found some hot stuff. Not that I was having orgasms any more frequently, but I certainly was enjoying myself. I watched couples getting each other off, or rather the woman getting the man off. Though it was very one-sided, it was still

titillating. I especially liked to hear a man sigh or moan as
the woman continued to arouse him. The more I heard men
grow excited, the more I could use that in my head when I
wanted to climax later. Why didn't I masturbate while
watching the porn? Sitting at my desktop computer didn't
lend itself to that. I needed to be able to lie down and get
comfortable. My orgasmic success was still unpredictable,
but I was finding new avenues to explore.

Two months after purchasing my first sex toy, I
became completely desensitized. But I wasn't giving up.
This time I went back to The Pleasure Chest with the
intention of buying a dildo. Still feeling embarrassed and
self-conscious, I wanted to make my exit out of there as
soon as possible, though, like the prior time, the
saleswoman exhibited patience and explained the
differences between them. I bought a new porn DVD and a
large dildo, and could hardly wait to get home to try out my
new purchases.

Yeah Baby - 2011

The dildo didn't fit! I could barely get it inside me. I felt certain I had made the wrong choice, that my eyes had been bigger than my vagina and that the dildo was too large for me. The Pleasure Chest had a strict no-return policy, so I was stuck with it.

I didn't know what I was going to do with an $80 dildo that didn't fit, but to my surprise, after trying it a few times my body adapted. And one night, with the dildo inside me, I stimulated my clit to orgasm and not just any orgasm, but something so powerful that it vibrated from the top of my head down my entire body, including my toes. My brain actually felt numb, in a good way. I had to tell Lisa about it, and my therapist. It was just too remarkable not to share. Another night I had two orgasms, one right after the other. If only I could bottle this!

On the free porn site, I stumbled across a clip that I watched many times. The way the man moaned and sighed affected me immensely. I discovered I loved watching a man cum and hearing his expression of release so much that I wanted to get inside the video myself. I wanted to be the woman pleasuring him.

And then came *the* video, the one I would take notes on, the one I would recite to each new man after which I'd be told I was amazing. You don't see the man's face. You only see his hard cock and a nude woman sitting on the bed, stroking it with both hands. What made it so erotic was what she said as she stroked his cock. She never licked it, sucked it, or fucked it. She just talked.

The woman had evidently prepped him ahead of time that there would be a fantasy woman involved in addition to her. And then she began.

"Do you want the head of your cock inside her pussy?" she asked.

"Yeah, baby," he responded.

"That feel good?"

"Yeah, baby."

And it went on from there. His deep voice was not loud, but you could tell he was already under her seductive powers. It was hot!

One day, after I had watched this scene for the umpteenth time, I clicked a section on the porn site called "Meet and Fuck." It took me to a website that very quickly asked me to sign up and pay money. There was no way in hell I was going to sign my name to anything. Didn't you get jailed for that sort of thing? I told my therapist about it, and he assured me you only got arrested for child porn.

And then he mentioned that there were *free dating sex websites.* I filed that under: potentially useful information. That night I searched the web and sure enough I found two, Flirthut.com and Benaughty.com.

Each time I took a new step in my sexual exploration I became fearful. What was I getting myself into? Was I going to get into trouble? Yet despite my fears, I realized I had to push the boundaries. To utter the words that were in my mind and forbidden: cock, pussy, cum, fuck. It was freeing—no, exhilarating! Walls were breaking down. No longer was I going to be constricted by what I was supposed to think, supposed to do, supposed to feel. I wanted to be free.

Sex Education – 1954

When I was twelve I had my first experience with sexual attraction. My parents were thinking of selling our house. We lived in a modest development in Sherman Oaks, so my mother made an appointment with a real estate agent to come over and give an estimate of what it might sell for. I remember the chair he sat in, and while my mother went to get him a cold drink, he asked me several questions. I noticed that he was good looking and from the interest he took in me I thought he was attracted to me. I was still so very young and not adept at hiding my feelings in front of my mother, so after he left I shared my observation with her.

"That's ridiculous," she said. "You're only twelve."

Shame washed over me. Embarrassment followed. At that moment I learned that I had better not trust what I saw or felt.

Maybe my comment about the real estate agent

prompted "the talk" because a few days later my mother asked me to join her on the patio. She said she had something to discuss with me. We sat opposite one another. It was a beautiful summer day. It would have been a good day to go swimming or play with my friend Penny.

"I think it's time for me to tell you about men and woman, and how babies are made."

I sensed she was uncomfortable and that she would rather have been making her famous pecan rolls, or really doing anything at all rather than sitting there with me.

"When a man and woman have sex," she began, "he inserts his penis into the woman's vagina." Her eyes moistened. I could feel my own eyes fill as well. "Like this," she added, and gave a crude demonstration, a straight finger of one hand inserting itself into the thumb and forefinger of the other hand. "The woman has something called a hymen and that means she's a virgin. The penis breaks through the hymen when they have sex."

A tear rolled down my mother's face. I reacted to her tears with tears of my own. Pretty soon we were crying and I had no idea why. My twelve-year-old mind concluded sex must be very unpleasant for a woman to endure. And I was already shutting down this part of myself after my mother's comment about the real estate agent.

"Women don't like sex," said my mother, which confirmed my thinking. "It's a woman's obligation to have sex with her husband to satisfy him."

"Oh." That's all I could say. *Can I go now and play*

with Penny?

"A woman bleeds every month. It's called a period. You will get your period within the next year or so, and when a woman gets pregnant her period stops until she has the baby. Then her period starts again."

"Oh," I repeated.

"Do you understand what I'm saying?"

"Uh-huh."

"Nice Jewish girls, good girls, don't have sex until they're married. Boys will want to, but good girls never do."

I said nothing.

"Do you have any questions?"

I shook my head. I had no curiosity about sex after the talk, no interest in it at all. I might have had an interest if she hadn't explained that it was so unpleasant. Why would I be interested in engaging in something that brought such discomfort? It seemed like such a secret, private talk that it didn't occur to me to talk to my friend Penny about it.

Decades later I was struck with the realization that I had never seen my mother cry at any other time throughout her entire life; not during her numerous hospitalizations, not when she gave herself insulin shots, not when she was dying. Only then, while giving me the talk.

Sex Appeal – 1956

My parents wanted to build their own home, so they bought a piece of property in Encino, which was further out in The Valley, in a less developed area than where we had been living. There were other new homes being built on our street. The neighborhood would grow quickly. I enjoyed watching the process of our house being built from the ground up.

After the foundation and framework were completed, I was able to locate my room, see how the furniture would be laid out, and take in the view through my large bedroom windows. I could also hike with my dog in the hills behind the house. A pool was excavated, fruit trees were planted, and a badminton court installed. All in all, this occupied my parent's minds for a while and they spent less time focusing their negativity on me and what I wasn't doing or what I was saying that might have offended their sensibilities.

The neighborhood wasn't the only thing that was developing. At fourteen I began to fill out a sweater. I got my first bra, pair of heels, and my period. I felt unusual stirrings in my body and I was looking at boys in a different way than before—and they were looking back.

Though I loved the piano, I didn't like learning classical music. My mother found a teacher for me who taught popular songs. His name was Blaine. I loved the music, and I adored him. He had a great personality and was fun to be with, and he praised me frequently. I could hardly wait until each lesson.

My parents enrolled me in Birmingham Junior High, which was still in army barracks, not having been rebuilt since World War II. After a couple of years, I was invited to join a club of girls. I was finally being accepted, but I never totally let my guard down, at home or at school. I could never let anyone know what really went on inside my mind, so I mostly listened to what everyone else was saying and nodded a lot. Also, I felt bound by a pact with my parents, unconsciously agreed to, that had *secret* written all over it. They could denigrate me, and I would accept it and not tell a living soul about it. For this I got to live under their roof.

My first musings about boys began at this time with the girls in the club. One of the girls would call attention to a boy who was handsome and we'd all agree. Another would mention a boy who was nerdy and we'd all agree. But a frank sexual discussion never took place. I had no sexual feelings that I was aware of, except for the desire to kiss the married doctor who lived across the street. Luckily for me my parents asked him to be my physician. If I got a cold, Mark would come to the house and attend to me. Being ill had its perks!

Starter Sex Continued - 2012

The first sex site I started with was Flirthut.com. This is where I had met Dave, who I mentioned earlier.

The process for signing up was simple. It asked you to fill out a profile, including sexual likes and dislikes, your age, where you lived, and a moniker for your screen name. Unlike regular dating sites, it did not ask for your profession, how much money you made, or to list the six things you could never live without. I signed up as *Sensualnights16* and listed my age as sixty-three, although I was actually sixty-nine. I rationalized that the further away from seventy I was, the more men I would interest. This was the only thing I lied about. Many men did not post a picture, and—not wanting my face shown on a sex site—in the photo I posted of myself I was wearing a hat that was pulled down over my eyes. All it showed were my lips, chin, and breasts underneath a T-shirt. I used the same picture on both sites, even though the ages I listed were different. As far as I know, no one ever noticed.

After hearing stories from Lisa about her young men, I decided to continue my dialogue with Dave if he contacted me. I told myself if I was uncomfortable I could always break it off.

~

Since our first chat, I thought about Dave a lot, picturing us meeting for a drink, having sex for real. And then I imagined a *relationship* with Dave, meeting his friends, and—wait a minute, was I completely out of my mind? I reminded myself that I had a sixty-year-old—all right, almost seventy-year-old—body, and he claimed to have a thirty-three-year-old body. I could fantasize a meet-and-greet all I wanted, but that's all it would ever be, a fantasy. It was *all* a fantasy. I had no idea if the person on the other end was young, old, incarcerated, or free. Nor did they know anything about me. I should say that if I liked a man, I did give my first name if he asked—but only if he asked. A friend suggested I might be communicating with an underage child or even a woman because anything is possible on the internet. But I had no doubt that Dave was anything but an adult male. I continued to focus on my exploration and pleasure.

I decided I needed to make more connections to avoid being focused on one man. Not having received many emails on Flirthut.com, I joined another sex site: Benaughty.com. This time though, when I got to the question of age, I lied and listed my age as forty-five. I wanted to see if the lower age would make a difference and it did. I received little interest on Flirthut.com, but I was flooded with requests to chat on Benaughty.com. I didn't like lying, particularly by stretching my age to this degree, but I wanted some attention, wanted to engage in online sex, and believed I wouldn't hurt anyone because I would never meet the person. So what was the harm? The men would be satisfied by my chat, and I would have some excitement.

I searched for the type of man I'd be interested in: intelligent, professional, sexy. I'd send a note if one aroused my curiosity, "Do you like naughty chat?" Most wrote back that they did. Some looked like serial killers with their stern expressions, intense eyes, and intimidating frowns. It was one thing to act out my prurient desires on a website; it was another to open myself up to a potentially unstable person. I rejected all men who weren't smiling.

There was something satisfying about getting a man excited and having him cum while chatting with me. Whatever else they might be lying about, I believed and trusted the fact that they were completely aroused. Somehow the men even managed to stroke themselves to orgasm and still type, up to and including, *"I'm cummmmmmming."*

Warming Up - 2012

I found a man on Benaughty.com who took communications up a level from Dave. He called himself R.C. and he was from North Carolina.

"What are you wearing?" he wrote.

I decided to tell the truth. "Sleeveless top and lightweight pants. It's very hot here."

"Home alone?" he asked.

"Yes."

"Then we're overdressed."

This one had a sense of humor. I liked that. He went about things slowly, and I liked that too. And despite the fact that this was on the internet and not in person, it was still sexy.

"I'm going to be working my fingers in and out of your pussy as you start to sway and moan. I want to lick your clit and suck it. I want you hot, wet, and cumming."

Before I got online, I'd had two glasses of wine and I

was buzzed. Because of it I was more aroused than normal, which is to say pretty aroused. I'd never had a man say to me, "I want you hot, wet, and cumming." Reading those words created a heightened desire in me and an openness to explore sex in a way I had never explored it before.

"I want to give you long licks from the bottom all the way up to your clit, using my hands to massage your ass as I tease your wet pussy, kneading your pussy lips, pulling them apart as my tongue fucks your pussy."

"Do it, baby."

"Lock your legs over my shoulders baring all to me as my cock goes deep inside you. I'm pounding against you as you moan and quiver beneath me, then driving in hard, filling your pussy, stretching it, punishing it."

"Fill me up, baby," I wrote. I was getting the hang of this.

So raw. So graphic. So forbidden. So exciting.

I was on an exhilarating ride and I didn't want to get off. In fact, I wanted to explore with R.C. and other men the dynamics of my sexuality. How far could I take this? How far was I willing to take this?

His Name Was Troy - 2012

In between switching back and forth between sex chats on Benaughty.com and Flirthut.com, I was still looking for a relationship on regular dating websites, OkCupid and POF.com (Plenty of Fish). I found Troy on Plenty of Fish. I had a measured attraction to him. I say "measured" because it was not like Larry or Shane, where I'd felt an immediate and powerful attraction, but I found his looks somewhat appealing. I wrote him and he wrote back and provided his phone number.

Troy was sixty-five. He asked me if I'd like to meet him for a drink. I said yes, and we set up a date and time. He suggested we make it in the afternoon. That way if we liked each other we could continue the date into the evening.

Even though the attraction wasn't strong, I was still looking forward to having a date with a real man. I looked at internet sex as a filler, "filler fantasy" was what I coined it, until I found the real thing.

We were to meet at a place called The Beach Club. I pictured, well, a beach club—tropical atmosphere thick with palm trees and exotic drinks—but when I arrived I saw that it was in fact a sports bar.

Observation Number 1: Doesn't belong to a beach club.

As I exited my car I noticed a man, reed thin and balding, heading toward the restaurant. My mind raced to think up a good excuse to end the date quickly.

Reluctantly, I kept walking toward the restaurant and saw another man waiting by the door. He looked at me, I looked at him, and I realized to my relief this was the guy. I confessed I'd thought my date was the previous man and he asked if I was disappointed. "Definitely not!" I answered.

Contrary to some previous experiences I'd had with online dating, where the man was so much worse looking than his picture, this man was infinitely better looking. I couldn't quite get over it and kept staring at him. Somehow, I think I feared that if I stopped looking at him, he might turn into some freakish character from a bad Hollywood movie.

I had fantasized ordering a martini on my way over, but martinis are expensive in Los Angeles, usually $12 or more, so I decided I would only order one if he did. He requested beer. So I ordered wine.

We did the first-date banter two-step until he told me he was an only child. I thought that was fairly unusual since I was an only child also. When I pointed that out he argued it wasn't unusual at all.

Observation Number 2 – Picks argument right off the bat.

He had moved to Los Angeles from San Francisco a year before and labeled Southern Californians *flaky* (I hadn't heard that term in decades), and also not very *intelligent.* My blood started to boil.

Observations Numbers 3 & 4 – Makes generalizations and is negative.

I was pissed off and intrigued at the same time.

"Do you think you're still hot?" Troy asked.

I was thrown by this question. I thought he meant did I still want sex.

"I still have desires."

"No, I mean has anyone told you?" he corrected.

I remembered Larry telling me he thought I was sexy, and frankly, I was wishing I was with him at that moment instead of Troy. "Yes, I've been told." I was losing patience with this guy.

After two hours of exchanging banalities, he asked the waitress for the check and said he'd have to be going. I figured we wouldn't see each other again because he was ending the date abruptly.

"So I guess you don't think we're a match," I said, surprised to hear these words come out of my mouth.

He appeared stunned. "Not at all, I find you very attractive. I'd like to see you again. Do you have any plans over the next several days?"

"I think I have some free time." I was available the entire weekend, but I wasn't going to tell him that.

"Are you healthy?"

Am I healthy? Where did that come from? No date had ever asked me this question before. I thought of lying, but sooner or later he'd find out so I told him that I'd had several joints replaced: shoulders, hips, and knees. I considered saying, *I'm wonder woman of the geriatric set* but decided against it.

"Was it because of cancer?"

"Arthritis." The word hung in the air like a bad fart. I wanted to take it back, eviscerate it, make it evaporate, stomp on it. "You wouldn't know if I hadn't told you," I blurted out in a failed attempt to deflect the seriousness of having had eight major joint replacements. I knew my revelation had just put the ax on this relationship.

"So you've been through a lot."

His pretend compassion didn't fool me. This date was finished; we both knew it. And then he said, "What would you like to do when we see each other ... a movie?"

Huh? What had just happened? Could I have been wrong? "If we could find one we both like," I managed, recovering.

"We could always have sex," he joked.

"We could."

He wanted to see me again after all! So forget about his negativity. Forget the generalities. Maybe he was nervous. Maybe on a second date he'd be different. My inner coach said: *Give the guy a chance.*

Troy walked me to my car and, spontaneously, I gave him a hug and he hugged me back.

After three days passed I knew I wouldn't hear from him. Maybe if he hadn't learned about my medical history he would have contacted me. Having arthritis definitely didn't work in my favor.

I had to keep reminding myself of my better qualities so I wouldn't become depressed, which would have been easy to do. Not everyone would see it as a deal breaker, right? After all, I had wit, intelligence, sensitivity, empathy, sensuality, creativity, kissable lips, and a body made for sex (meaning I'm ready, willing and able)! And more! Take that, Troy!

I didn't tell him, and why would I, I didn't even know him, it didn't really affect me in bed. However, it is difficult for me to be on my knees very long in the woman on top position. I'm also uncomfortable having my neck suspended without support when performing fellatio, but there are many positions where I'm just fine.

Swine: That's the word that came to mind when I thought about Troy leading me on.

Observation Number 5 - Pay more attention to observations.

First Kiss – 1956

Boys were the subject of unending conversations with my girlfriends, but it was all very innocent. What was a real romantic kiss, like in the movies, going to feel like? How old would we be when it happened? I didn't know it, but I was about to find out.

I was becoming a young woman. My parent's friends often said I was pretty or beautiful. I liked how it felt and a new identity was forming.

In the spring of 1956, my parents took me to Highland Springs, California for a weekend vacation. The resort was located ninety minutes outside of Los Angeles on the way to Palm Springs. We had been there before, and I loved it. I had the chance to go horseback riding, swimming, eat good food, and enjoy some local entertainment.

This time there was a group of high school kids in addition to families. I was in my last year of junior high. One night, the resort held a gathering for teens in the recreation room. I attracted the eye of a sixteen-year-old boy named Jimmy. After Jimmy and I spent some time together talking, he asked me if I'd like to take a walk. Jimmy slid his arm around my waist as we left.

I remembered "the talk" from two years ago and what a nice girl did or didn't do with a boy. I had no intention whatsoever of doing anything other than what I thought was appropriate.

It was a warm, beautiful night, with many stars, and a big bright moon lighting up the path for us. Jimmy led me to a chaise lounge. We lay down and he kissed me. My first real, romantic kiss! It was nothing like "spin the bottle" a few years earlier, when the bottle I spun had stopped in front of an ugly boy I didn't know or care about. Jimmy was tall, had dark curly hair, and was very handsome. Wow, a boy I liked who also liked me! We kissed again. And then suddenly, from out of nowhere, I heard my father's booming voice, "Get up, Lynn." I disengaged from Jimmy, and saw my mother and father hovering over me.

"Get out of here," my father ordered Jimmy, and he ran off.

My father grabbed my arm and pulled me in the direction of our cabin.

"Nobody behaves like that unless she's a prostitute," my mother said.

"But we were only kissing!" I cried out.

I knew they didn't believe me. And they definitely didn't trust me. I found myself needing to prove that I was a decent person and a worthwhile person to my own parents.

There was no further dialogue. There was nothing more I could say or do. It was clear they weren't going to listen to me. I didn't know it then, but my training to suppress my sexual needs was now firmly in place, as well as the suppression of my thoughts and feelings.

We left the resort the next morning, two days earlier than planned.

Now I was certain that sex was bad. Was I bad too, even though I didn't have sex?

The Good Daughter – 1958

If I couldn't be a perfect child, I could at least strive to be a good one. What my parents thought of me meant the world to me. After all, if I wasn't accepted and loved by my own parents, who else in this world would ever love me?

One day I came home from school and found my mother passed out on the floor in the hallway.

"Mother!" I screamed. "Wake up! Wake up!"

After a couple moments, she came to. She had suffered a diabetic coma and asked me to bring her orange juice, which I did. The sugar in the orange juice helped her gain her equilibrium, allowing her to function again. She said she was going to call the doctor. There was anger in her voice. So I grew angry too.

I heard her talking to him from the other room. I picked up the extension. At fifteen, I was old enough and bold enough, I thought, to express myself. I was furious that he hadn't given her the help she needed, although not knowing what that might have been, so this episode wouldn't have happened to her. I raged against this doctor for letting this happen to my mother.

"Get off the line, Lynn," my mother demanded. Stung and surprised by her response, I hung up.

She came into my room afterward.

"Don't ever do that again," she said.

I thought she'd be proud of me for standing up for her. But she was enraged. I came to hate that doctor. I didn't think about hating her. I was too hurt. I never said another word against him or any other doctor of hers. Most of the time she revered her doctors. I was both jealous of the high regard she had for them, and incensed she had wound up in a coma that could have left me motherless if she had died. But I didn't dare bring that up.

Without realizing it, I shut down any free or spontaneous thinking, and kept whatever inner life I had to myself. I participated in conversations without ever really saying anything. From early on I became resolute that my parents would never really know me. The only problem was that I stifled who I was so thoroughly, that I didn't really know me either.

Dave Continued - 2012

I finally received another email from Dave. He wrote
he had been busy with college and work. I was
communicating with someone in college?

"How's your week been so far, and would you like to
chat a little?"

I wanted to chat more than a little! Thinking about
Dave sent a sexual current running throughout my body. I
wrote back, "Sure, what do you have in mind?"

He wrote back, "Any new pictures yet?"

I did not have any new pictures and told him so. What
men wanted were body shots.

I didn't want to send Dave a body shot. I didn't like
the way my body was photographing. I looked better in
person. Was a picture of my body a prerequisite to our
chatting again? I didn't like the demanding feel of it.

"If you're concerned, I'm a size 10." This was my
truthful size.

He wrote back, "Not concerned at all. Want to look at you when we chat."

Now I understood. He wanted to use it for visual stimulation. I still wasn't going to send him a body shot.

My thoughts were becoming preoccupied with Dave—maybe because he was my "first." Another three weeks passed with no communication from him so I decided to fill some of that time with a few new men who actually excited me more.

When I did chat with Dave again, it wasn't the same for me as the first few times. The new men were sophisticated, and funny, and older. Nick in Spokane, Washington described himself as 6' tall, with dark hair, and said he was an architect. Jim in Warrendale, Pennsylvania described himself as 5'10", blond, and a lawyer. Robert in Watertown, New York was 6'3", and a builder.

The fact that none of these men claimed to live in Los Angeles was fine with me. I went to Flirthut.com and Benaughty.com for sexual liberation and enjoyment, not to find a relationship, unlike with OkCupid and Plenty of Fish. What they were looking for? Casual sex was the norm, as well as oral-receiving and oral-giving, role playing, and erotic stories. I passed on those who said, kinky games. Maybe I was missing out on something, but I decided to go with what was comfortable for me, and let that lead the way.

My nights were suddenly filled up. Instead of watching mindless TV or reading yet another book, I was socializing and having fun, filling two voids, loneliness and sexual excitement.

R.C. - 2012

R.C. and I were about to have another encounter on Benaughty.com. I couldn't wait.

He had titillated me like no other so far. This time I wanted to titillate him. I planned to use the notes from my favorite porn clip. I told him I had a surprise for him. R.C. liked to dominate, and my story required that he lie back and let me handle things. Initially, he let me lead the way.

"This time there's going to be another woman joining us," I wrote.

"Excellent," he responded.

"She's tall, blond, and totally different from me."

"Can I touch you while she's involved?"

"Okay," I said, already anticipating that he wasn't going to let me lead him.

"I'm catching your clit between my finger and thumb, squeezing a little, rolling it back and forth."

"That feels good."

"I'm going to mount you as you lie spread out across the bed, holding you there to enjoy fucking your wet lips, forcing my cock in your hot pussy."

"Oh, yes."

"Starting to move steadily deeper, pulling back then thrusting harder, pumping my cock in and out of your pussy."

Using my notes was hopeless. He was intent on leading, so I just went along with it.

"Pumping you faster, filling you, stretching you."

"Yes, baby."

"Starting to move steadily deeper, pulling back then thrusting harder."

"Oh, that's so good."

"Wild, hard fucking … sweating, screaming, cussing, holding you impaled on my cock, forcing it in deeper. Wanting all of my cock inside you."

"I want all of it, too. Are you getting ready to cum, baby?"

"Yes. I'm gonna shoot a load in your tight pussy, your clit pulsating … AAAAAAAAAAAAA."

"Oh!" This was all I could manage, amazed at his ability to think this through and type, while at the same time stimulating himself to orgasm.

"That was awesome," wrote R.C.

"Yes, it was."

"I'm sorry I ruined your plans."

"What do you mean?" I asked.

"About the story you wanted to tell me. Your blond

friend is really going to be pissed."

I laughed. This guy was funny. And sensual. And sexy. And another one I wasn't going to meet.

At the conclusion of the experience, I felt elated to have had an exchange like this with a man—so spontaneous, so free to express myself in this graphic way. What had seemed so objectionable earlier in my life I now embraced.

The Messages Keep Coming In – 2012

"Naughty thunder is coming! Surrender! I'm too hot to resist!"

"Hey, your hot, naughty match is right here waiting. Distance doesn't matter to me. Let's just hang out and enjoy some fun moments."

These messages were anything but enticing.

"Hey, wait up ... how about meeting a hot man? If you're interested ask me anything you want and I'll show you the real meaning of fun!" This note came from a body that was anything but hot. This is what he wanted:

> The sitting in a chair position, the doggy style
> position, oral receiving, oral
> giving, take you from behind, rimming receiving,
> voyeurism, orgies,
> cock rings, clit stimulators, dildos, big clits, small
> tits, vibrators, swing,

blindfolds, wild games on first date, adult movies at
home, swinging
parties, visiting specialty shops, erotic stories,
playing with toys.

Some of these things were exciting to me, but many
were not, such as wild games on the first date, swinging,
orgies, and rimming. I scratched Naughty Thunder off my
list of potential chat-mates. His approach might have been
great for someone else, but it wasn't comfortable for me.

I continued to chat with others though, and there were
a few men I liked who wanted to meet me in person. I was
tempted, but I'd have to tell them I was twenty-five years
older than I'd claimed on the site. I even had fantasies that
this would be okay with them. My rationale was that
because the online sex had been so good for them, they
would understand and forgive me. Sure. On the other
hand, I had nightmares of them being so angry with me that
they would try to get back at me in some way, enticing me
to meet them somewhere and then inflicting some horrible
punishment on me. And not the erotic, *Story of O* or *Fifty
Shades of Grey* kind of punishment either. Being an older
woman, and having had many joint replacements, if true
danger were present I could not run or fight back.

I was receiving no messages on Flirthut.com, where
my stated age was sixty-three, but continued to receive
daily messages from many men on Benaughty.com, where
my age was forty-five. Thinking back, ironically, at forty-
five when men were most attracted to me I was repressed

and embarrassed to let myself delve into my sexuality. Now I was breaking out of my shell—a positive thing that had come with aging—yet at the same time, as an older woman I was so often invisible.

R.C. – 2012

R.C. continued to have sex chats with me.

"Slowly, I rock my hips and slide the head of my hard cock back and forth over your clit."

"Oh, God, that feels so good," I responded in writing.

"You try to push down to swallow my cock in your wet pussy. I begin to suck your nipples as I slow fuck between your pussy lips."

I didn't know I could get so aroused hearing a man talk to me that way." I couldn't get enough of him.

His profile said that he liked to read history, erotica, and biographies. I wanted to know more about him. Each time I went to Benaughty.com I looked to see if he had sent me a message, and was disappointed when he hadn't.

R.C.'s moniker was *Sharp Mind with Slow Hands*. I wished those slow hands were on me. We connected a few times a week, and I fantasized having sex with him in person often.

With each sexual exchange I was becoming more liberated, closer to finding my sexual core. That I could communicate with someone in an openly sexual way after being so closed off was exciting and inspiring.

The picture R.C. posted was of himself on a powerboat. He was tall and had sandy-colored hair. I asked him about his boat and he said he took it out at a nearby lake. I wrote a story to send to him, a fantasy of what it might be like if I was out on that boat with him.

BELOW DECK:

It is the start of the summer season. We are dressed for a day on the lake, which is to say we're wearing very little. Just enough to be legal. The sun is streaming down upon us and the wind is whipping through our hair. Riding the waves with you and being cooled by the lake's spray is a sensual experience, and we can't help but think about later. We smile at each other and bide our time.

After several hours, when we return from our adventure, another awaits us below deck. As usual, I make us vodka tonics. We take the first sips of our drinks and then you reach for me. You press your body up against mine. You're already hard. I start to slide down your body.

"Let me take a shower, baby," you say.

"No, I want you just the way you are."

My hand finds your stiff cock. I stroke it a little but waste no time unzipping your shorts. I tug at your dick and free it. I kneel down on the cabin floor and take the head of your cock in between my lips tasting your precum as my darting tongue flicks the tip.

I suck you good and hard and I want you to cum but you stop me and guide me to the bed. "You know what I want first." I open my legs to your eager mouth. Your soft lips are on my clitoris. Once you start your gentle but insistent sucking, I am your captive. I want to hold out, but you work your magic on me. You bring heaven and earth to me as I erupt in long, rolling waves but you don't stop, encouraging me with your mouth to keep cumming until the very last sensation leaves my body. Only when you're sure I'm sated do you enter me and give me the ultimate pleasure.

Summer is my favorite season. Our after-boating pleasure is always hot. We grill some chicken for dinner and when we're full, we return below deck. The shower is barely big enough for one, let alone two. But we like to finish off the day lathering each other up and toweling each other off. And then we have a go at our version of dessert.

But, alas, I didn't send the fantasy. Maybe I'd send it when I got to know him a little better.

Ties That Blind – 1957

In summer, my mother would sometimes sit out by the pool with me. She would tell me how badly she felt about her thighs. They were distorted, a very large lump of fat had settled in when she lost over one hundred pounds right after my birth. Losing a dramatic amount of weight quickly is a symptom of diabetes that prompted a doctor's visit and led to my mother learning that she had the disease.

In an effort to make her feel better, I persuaded her to look at my thighs, pointing out that mine were fat and unattractive, and hers were no worse. I was often ten pounds overweight so I had some small basis on which to offer the comparison. This was the dance we engaged in every summer, just the two of us. Ever mindful of needing to prop her up emotionally, I was at the ready with a compliment or something positive to say to make her feel better. Bolstering her up by diminishing myself seemed to improve her spirits. I didn't realize that I resented doing this.

At night, I would have a recurring nightmare that my parents were sitting side-by-side in attached wooden chairs suspended by a crane. The crane holding the chairs would become loose, and suddenly my parents dropped to their deaths. I'd wake up terrified of my urge to kill them.

Shaken, needing something to calm myself down, I'd go to the freezer and eat a few of my mother's homemade chocolate chip cookies. They were delicious frozen.

We'd be having breakfast the next morning when my mother would announce that some of the chocolate chip cookies were gone.

"Who ate them?" she'd demand.

By virtue of her asking the question, not to mention the accusatory tone, I was convinced I'd done the wrong thing.

"Not me," I lied.

I wasn't about to confess eating four chocolate chip cookies without knowing the penalty. I don't know why she would inspect the frozen can of cookies before breakfast, but she had an uncanny ability to ferret out whatever she could use to make me feel ashamed.

Every move, every thought, every expression was cause for examination. Something as pedestrian as how I set the table was subject to review. I knew as long as I was under my parent's tutelage I'd be under a microscope.

Sam – 2012

Sam from Australia contacted me through Flirthut. I opened up his profile, and the first thing I saw was a huge erect penis. After seeing that photo, I reached out to him.

My appetite for sex was growing, and if I couldn't have it in real life, I was sure as hell going to have it online.

We had one very intense sex chat that ended abruptly. The next day I received this message from Sam: "Hi, sorry for leaving so quickly. My wife woke up!"

"Thanks for letting me know," I responded. "I didn't know you were married ... had fantasies of us having wild sex one day!"

"Who knows, we could still."

Sam had sent me some cock shots and a video of him cumming. I had to wait to see it on Lisa's computer because mine was too old. The video was very erotic, showing him masturbating, then cumming. I was discovering the voyeuristic side of me, and I was enjoying it!

I sent Sam a photo that emphasized my full lips.

"I love your luscious lips, wish they were on my cock to wake me up," Sam wrote.

I wrote him, "I was so wet after our chat. I don't think I've ever been that wet before."

Telling a man I was wet, that I desired his cock in my mouth, engaging with men in this way—this was exhilarating. Walls were breaking down.

"Mmmm. Love that. I'm horny again," he said.

I received one more email from Sam.

"I'm leaving this site – sorry – you can contact me on email if you want."

I did email Sam to try to continue our chats but he said he'd decided not to go forward, that he felt guilty toward his wife. I wrote him back that I thought it was great that he had a conscience and wished him good luck. And I meant it. But I missed my sexy Aussie.

THE SEMINAR – CIRCA 2012

A Short Story

I met Rod on Benaughty.com. He lived in Kansas.
We exchanged some steamy chats and then moved to
private email. Around this same time, a writer friend of
mine gave me some erotica to read and suggested I write an
erotica story for a contest she was planning on entering.
Write an erotic story? I didn't think I could do it, but I
decided to try. Reading erotica was a powerful aphrodisiac
for me, but I found writing erotica even more pleasurable,
as it enabled me to tap deeper still into my sensuality. I felt
creative with Rod and began sending him stories I would
invent for the two of us to enjoy.

THE SEMINAR

My friends all envied me for being able to leave

Los Angeles and "jet" (their term) across the country for a weekend seminar on real estate in New York. But I would rather have stayed home and worked. I had a few really good prospects who were looking for homes, and I didn't know if they'd hang around and wait for me until I returned on Monday.

One girlfriend even suggested I might meet someone. Like I was really in the mood for that. My boyfriend of two years and I had a recent parting of the ways due to an innocent flirtation I had with a co-worker. He interpreted it as having far more significance than it actually had. Maybe I was searching for something and didn't realize it. Well, I wasn't going to think about it now. I had what was probably going to be a boring seminar to attend, with some real estate guru, about how to generate international business. Was I really that ambitious? At this point, I would have loved to kick off my heels and have a good night's sleep. More clients, be damned!

~

The hotel awakened me early per my request. I wanted to make sure I had time for a substantial breakfast and plenty of coffee. I figured they would keep me from falling asleep, which I had done at other seminars due to a lack of protein or caffeine. I wasn't going to take my chances; I had both.

In the ballroom and seated by 8:45, fifteen minutes early, I rechecked my lipstick, scanned the program, and still had time to kill.

I took a cursory look around the room and our eyes met. After a brief surge of sexual current flowed through my body, I lowered my eyes to my notepad, jotting something down to make myself look like I had an important thought. When I raised my eyes, I intended to look straight ahead of me, at the head of the person in front of me, or at the stage. Anywhere but back at you. But my eyes drifted over, and this time our gaze held. You smiled and I smiled back. I think I giggled a little. I felt like I was back in high school.

I had paid a lot of money for this seminar and I intended to get as much out of it as possible, but after the guru made his first joke to warm up the room, I cooled off. I couldn't keep my eyes from training on yours. We were on clear opposite sides of the room. There was no way we could *accidently* bump into each other, or casually move to sit next to one another. Somehow we remained stationary until the lunch break at noon.

It was a relief to stand up and stretch my legs. Three hundred other people rose also, and were making their way to the assorted hotel restaurants. I had no idea if I'd see you. I knew I had to get food in me to last through the afternoon. I heard a baritone voice say, "Hello."

I turned. It was you.

"Hi." You held out your hand.

"Hi," I said, shaking it. As we touched I felt an instant connection to you. I noticed the grey flecks in your hair which I couldn't see at a distance, and a five o'clock shadow even though it was only noon. I figured you had to be in your late forties, somewhere in the neighborhood of thirteen or so years my junior. Someone my height usually wasn't attractive to me, but you were the exception. You were very self-assured and that intrigued me.

"Would you like to get some lunch?"

"That would be lovely."

The feel of your hand on the small of my back was electrifying. You guided me to the main dining room, but there was a long line.

"We can get a drink and order food over there," you said, gesturing to the bar, but when we arrived and looked around, we saw all the tables had already been taken.

I kept looking at your mouth. It quivered, but not nervously. It was very sexual, like you'd rather be doing something else with it outside of talking or eating. I wanted you right then and there.

"At the risk of sounding inappropriate, we could get room service in my suite. It's quite large, with chairs and a table.

"Let's," I said, without hesitation.

In spite of the wall-to-wall bodies in the elevator, we never took our eyes off each other. I knew this was crazy - going up to a man's room so quickly - but I didn't care. I hadn't felt such a powerful attraction to anyone in a long time. Suddenly, I wasn't hungry, and I didn't care about the seminar or all the money I had spent.

We entered your suite. It looked more like a home than a hotel room, high ceilings, lush furniture, and full bar.

"May I take your jacket?" you asked. I let it slide off my shoulders and into your hands. I felt your warm breath on my neck, and it was intoxicating. You turned me around to face you, then leaned in to kiss me.

"Do you want lunch first?" you whispered.

"No," I answered.

Your kissing became more passionate.

You pulled me toward you and rubbed up against me. Your erection spoke of the promise of imminent ecstasy. Reflectively, I let out a huge sigh. I could feel my panties were already damp.

"C'mon," you said, guiding me toward the bed. As we removed each other's clothes, you took my nipple in your mouth. I pushed down on your shoulders and, reading my signal, you lowered yourself down my body. As you began sucking on my clit I cried out. Nothing had ever felt that good and I was sure nothing ever would again. Somewhere in my head I realized I didn't even know your name, but I didn't care. You worked my clit like I imagined a pro would do, licking it, tugging at it, all with a gentle insistence, and driving me thoroughly crazy. As I held your head close to me, I came in pronounced waves in your mouth.

After I had a moment to absorb the joy of what had just happened, I kissed your chest, your belly, and your raging hardness. Your girth was impressive and sucking your hard shaft created an overpowering urge in me to have you inside me. But I wanted to give as good as I got so I tried to be patient, tried to hold myself back from just getting on that hard cock and riding you like a cowgirl.

"Come up here," you said. So now my patience was going to be rewarded. I noticed how really impressive your cock was as I lowered myself onto you. I loved how it stretched my pussy. I made sure I looked you in the eyes as I slid up and down that hard dick. Your breathing increased and I felt you were close.

"Give me all you've got, baby," I said.

You moaned loudly and shot your load into me, crying out, "Fuck! Oh, fuck!"

I loved that you were loud, so virile, so in the throes of pure lust. It was beautiful.

I'd never seen a man recover so fast. Before I knew it, we were at it again. We decided to skip the rest of the seminar and fuck each other all weekend. I never learned your name, or whether you were married or single. I don't even remember if we ate.

When my friends asked me how the seminar was, I told them it was by far the best investment I ever made in myself.

Into the Abyss - 1957

I tried desperately not to offend my parents, and struggled to stay out of their crosshairs, but I simply wasn't quick enough. I'd veer to the left, then to the right, but my parents were very good shots, aiming their fire for everything wrong in their lives straight for my heart. My mental stability was at stake, and sometimes I held on by only a thread.

There was a period of time in my teens when I didn't kiss my mother goodnight, though I don't recall the reason. I kissed my father, but not my mother. Though he understood that I was angry with my mother, he never talked to me about it, never tried to uncover the motivation behind it, or serve as peacemaker. He just pinned the blame entirely on me.

Later in life, my father once told me that during that time, my mother expressed to him that she was afraid I would murder her in her sleep. I don't know why he told me that—perhaps to make me feel sorry for her or feel guilty. But that would never have happened anyway. If I had murdered her, it wouldn't have been in her sleep. I would have wanted her eyes wide open so she would be fully aware of what was unfolding.

The verbal assaults my mother, and sometimes my father, hurled at me crowded my mind. *Think, Lynn, think.* Lies were frowned upon, but the truth was unacceptable. *If I can't tell a lie and I can't tell the truth, what do I say?*

I grasped at any kindness that came my way. Simple birthday wishes were elevated to precious memory status and I'd replay them in my head repeatedly. The good days were so good and the bad days so bad, I couldn't make sense of it. Had I imagined the bad times? Or had I imagined the good ones? Having had sisters and brothers might have helped soften the blows; we could have compared notes. *What do you think? Is this for real?* A sibling might answer, "That's just Mom, that's just Dad, we're all going through it." But as it was, I had to fend for myself.

Deeper Into the Abyss - 1957

Shortly after I was born my mother developed diabetes. This disease is often inherited and goes from father to daughter, and from mother to son. But my mother told me it was because of my birth. From time to time, she'd remind me of this.

"Because of me? How?" I asked, horrified.

"The doctor said your birth was a shock to my system."

I didn't want to believe that I was to blame for such a horrible thing, a heavy weight for small shoulders to bear.

Once I became an adult, I asked a doctor about this. He told me that an event like birth, can trigger something like diabetes, but it was unlikely. However, the way my mother described it, it was an irrefutable connection. My mother meant it to have maximum impact on me, for me to feel guilt, and for decades I did.

One day my mother confided she had become pregnant

and that she had been so happy because she had always wanted more children. *What would she do with more children?* I wondered. *She can barely handle the one she's got.*

She was instructed by her doctor to get an abortion because otherwise she could die in childbirth. She told me she would have had twin boys. By her logic, I not only caused her diabetes but I had killed off my twin brothers, because if she hadn't gotten the diabetes then it would have been safe for her to give birth to her twin boys.

I wanted to empathize with her about the loss of the twins. That would have been my natural response. But the way she presented it to me, as if the twins would have been the key to her happiness, made me want to shut out her words and escape to somewhere where someone would find me to be enough.

I saw her as such an unkind woman, with a total lack of ability to nurture and love. All I could think of when she'd talk about it, which wasn't often, was that it was a blessing in disguise she hadn't had more children, callous as that may seem. Her story was one more weapon in the arsenal of many that she used to induce guilt and worthlessness. It would have been folly to bring more children into the world under her tutelage, and if she didn't realize it, maybe the greater powers that be did.

∾

Sometimes I was foolhardy. Sometimes I asked my mother about a decision she'd made in order to understand her better.

"You're aggravating me," she would warn. "The doctor said that I should not be aggravated."

I learned quickly that "aggravated" was code for: *I could go into a coma/be hospitalized/die* and *the doctor said* was code for "Leave me alone."* One of the places she wanted to be left alone was in the kitchen. She was so adamant so often about this I don't think it's any wonder that when I grew up I never wanted to learn to cook.

Often I felt shredded to pieces by my mother, but with the exception of an occasional fantasy, I did not want her to die. And I for sure didn't want that guilt on my head. It would have capsized my life with no hope of recovery. I could not let that happen. And yet, it seemed as if the situation was out of my control. Every move I made was magnified and molded into some meaning I didn't intend, all a threat to her, potentially causing her catastrophic consequences. I came to realize my very presence could be lethal. I was preoccupied with my mother dying. But that's easy to understand, I guess. My mother referred to the subject, directly or indirectly, daily. My father always believed my mother's life hung in the balance, and so he would never intervene or argue with what he believed was a fact in the life of a diabetic. And for the most part it was. But my mother played it up to the hilt every single day. As a result, my father and I were always on edge, from morning to night, hour by hour, minute by minute.

~

Years later, in my early twenties, my mother's car went off a cliff as she drove back over Coldwater Canyon from the city to The Valley. It didn't occur to me that my mother might be trying to harm herself until later that night, and it was never clear to anyone whether it was an accident or a suicide attempt. She emerged barely scathed, but she could easily have been killed, and she didn't express any relief or thankfulness that she was still alive or in one piece. One could almost get the sense that she was disappointed. Did she want to die? No one asked, least of all me (I would have been railed against for daring to bring it up), so it was left an unknown.

A friend recently asked me if there wasn't some kind of therapy available to her after the accident. Therapy was an explosive word in our family. Had it been mentioned, my mother would have flown into a rage. Neither my father nor mother had any respect for practitioners of the mind, let alone the idea of undergoing therapy with one. And at that time society was not generally accepting of those seeking psychological help. My parents reflected typical 1960s thinking: that people seeking counseling were "weak" and weak was the last label my parents wanted attached to them.

From time to time I did aggravate my mother

unintentionally and worried terribly. Would I, by
inadvertently upsetting her, send my mother to her death?
Or would she die by her own hand? I'd go to bed
wondering if I'd wake up to find her dead. Whatever the
reason, I knew most likely I would be to blame.

A Star Was Born – 1958

My father ran his upholstery business for years by himself; it was backbreaking work. My mother, eager to relieve him of the burden of lifting and carrying furniture, suggested they go into business together and become interior designers. That neither of them knew anything about interior design was not considered a hindrance. They would teach themselves. They leased a store on Ventura Boulevard in the heart of the business district of The Valley. My father, grateful for my mother's benevolence, insisted the store be named after her: *Muriel Brown Interior Design.* He also recognized that she needed to be the star. He hired the best signage company available, and when darkness fell, my mother's name lit up the boulevard. Now everyone would know Muriel Brown.

They made a good team. They worked side-by-side, honing their craft and becoming very successful, though there were always problems to overcome. Even when there

was a surplus of clients, a fabric a customer ordered could
be out of stock or delayed for months, or the order would
come in on time but it would be the wrong fabric and had
to be sent back. In each case, my parents had to give the
client the option of cancelling the order. If they lost the
customer, they'd have to start all over again with someone
new. But mostly the orders kept coming in, and they were
in need of extra help.

Two close girlfriends of mine, both age sixteen, were
hired by my parents to work part-time. One would come in
Monday, Wednesday, and Friday and the other Tuesday,
Thursday, and Saturday. My mother told me how much
she liked having the girls working at her side. "They can't
do enough for me."

She needed to be idolized, and my girlfriends catered
to that need. I never understood why she had to be
worshipped, and particularly by my friends. Why wasn't
my love enough? Or maybe it wasn't love I was giving,
maybe it was obedience. It was difficult to give my mother
love. It was only good when it came from other people.

At one point my parents made overtures for me to join
them in the business. My first response was a silent one.
*Are they insane? Do they really think I would want to work
for them?* I was easily intimidated by my parents but this
time was the exception. I stood my ground and told them I
was not interested in interior design. I didn't confess the
greater truth: that there was no way in hell I was going into
business with them, that I may as well have slit my wrists,
that if I were to build my future in their business, I would

never have a leg of independence to stand on ever again.

My father and mother were inseparable. They did everything together. He would have his clients and she would have hers, but they consulted each other on every aspect of the showroom and design jobs, so working there would have deepened my entrapment. About four or five in the afternoon, they would have cocktails together and discuss their day, and then go out to dinner together. As if that wasn't enough, there were her health issues and their obsession with them. Most were related to her disease, but some were not.

Once, when we were visiting relatives in Chicago and enjoying a nice dinner of roasted chicken and mashed potatoes at an aunt's apartment, mother got a chicken bone caught in her throat and had to be rushed to the hospital. We waited, hearts in mouths, for word on her condition. My father always expected the worst, and taking my cue from him, so did I. She made it through, but it was always a life and death event when it came to my mother.

No, for the sake of my sanity there was no way I could have worked with them. I needed all the space I could get.

～

Occasionally, when business was slow and my mother's condition took a serious downturn, my father would tell me, "We might have to sell the house to pay for your mother's medical insurance, but don't say anything yet."

Of course, my mother would have to be informed if that happened, but at that moment he didn't want to burden her. So I carried the burden. Another secret for me to keep. I remember the uncertainty. *Will we have a roof over our heads? What will happen to us if we don't?*

Yet somehow, through it all, the house was never sold and mother would often receive a piece of jewelry for her birthday, or possibly a fox stole or mink coat on their anniversary, followed by three weeks in Hawaii to celebrate. I wondered, *If we're so poor how can we afford this?* For a period of time my father wouldn't bring it up so I figured we were okay.

And then, out of the blue, "We might have to sell the house," he would say, starting the whole cycle all over again.

My First Time – 1960

I had just begun working at my first real job, for
Encyclopedia Americana. The company's offices were
over the hill from The Valley, and I enjoyed the drive and
putting some distance in between my parents and myself.
At eighteen, I was the freshest face there, and the handsome
man in charge of the sales department came over to flirt
with me. Duane was ten years older than me, and
charming. With his deep dimples and beautiful smile,
Duane was sexy, no doubt about it. He reminded me of the
actor William Holden, whom I'd had a crush on ever since
watching the film *Picnic* and the erotic dance scene in
which he and Kim Novak snapped their fingers to the
music and made love with their eyes.

I had never even seen a man's penis before, much less
had sex. The only time I had ever kissed a man in a truly
romantic way was that one brief instance with Jimmy at
Highland Springs Ranch Inn, when my parents found me

on the chaise lounge and eviscerated my life.

But again, like with Jimmy, I felt totally in control of my sexuality. I was as indoctrinated as if I had taken sacred vows of chastity. I was saving myself for my husband and that was that.

One night Duane said he'd really like to show me his apartment. I made it clear I didn't want to have sex, and he said he said he was okay with that. He picked me up from my parent's house and we drove to Glendale. I did not tell my parents where we were going. I had complete confidence in myself that I wouldn't have sex, but I also knew my parents. If they thought there might be a man, a bed, and me in one place, it would have ignited a full-blown uproar.

After we were in his apartment for a few minutes, he said, "Let's lie down on the bed and hold each other."

"Remember what you promised me?" I answered, feeling strength in my conviction.

"I know," said Duane. "I remember."

I was not aroused. I had my mind under control and didn't feel tempted at all.

"I really need you, baby."

I started to pull away from him and get off the bed.

"Come back, baby. I won't do anything."

So I lay back down again. He took my hand and placed it on his penis, which I could tell through his clothing was stiff. Still it had no impact on me.

"What if I just put it inside you a little? Not so much though that you wouldn't be a virgin anymore."

"I don't know," I said, shaking my head.

"Please baby? I really need you." He gazed at me with longing eyes.

"I would still be a virgin?" I asked, the question floating in the air, along with the musk from his aftershave.

"Yes, baby, I'll show you."

He unzipped his pants and took it out. I don't remember thinking or feeling anything but fear. I didn't notice if it was large or small, and I wouldn't have known the difference anyway. I was just terrified he would break my hymen, that I would get pregnant, and that my parents would be so stunned and disapproving of me that they would want nothing more to do with me. I felt tenuously connected to them as it was.

I had no real understanding of sex from the limited education I'd received from my mother. My father never talked to me about sex either, only about boys in general. "Boys will try to take advantage of you in any way they can. They'll tell you anything so that you'll give in to them. I know, I was a boy once. Mark my words, Lynn. Don't do it! You'll be sorry afterward."

So I let Duane put it in me. It hurt and I didn't feel aroused at all. I didn't want it inside me. I didn't like it. He made a few small thrusting motions and a few seconds later he pulled out and masturbated to climax.

We did this several more times in the course of our relationship. I did it for Duane. Like my mother said, I did it to please him. I was just happy when I got my period every month and that I was still a virgin. My mother had told me that even a single drop of semen on your thigh could get you pregnant. I wasn't aware of any semen ever being on my thigh, but I was so naïve that I didn't know anything except what Duane told me—all of which I believed, unquestioningly.

One Sunday during the summer, Duane was over for a pool party my parents were having for their friends. We wound up in the house at the same time. I went into the bathroom, and he followed me. He tried to have sex with me but I told him no. I told him I was afraid of having sex so often, reminding him that I wanted to remain a virgin.

He rolled his eyes at me. "You're not a virgin, and you weren't a virgin before we ever got together!" he said sarcastically.

"I was a virgin! And what do you mean? You told me I was still a virgin," I protested, tears forming in my eyes.

"You've had sex before," he answered.

"I have not! I've never had sex!" I said, blindsided by his accusation.

"C'mon, who're you kidding?"

"I have never … had … sex … before," I said, emphatically. *This can't be happening. This can't be true. How could he do this to me? Oh my God, what have I done?*

I didn't have sex for three years after that. I felt so betrayed; horrified that he had lied to me, mortified that I had believed him, and deeply ashamed that I had lost my virginity and that I'd lost it in the way I had, by a liar and a manipulator.

Who will want to marry me now?

Confusion – 1962

Lines were beginning to blur. I didn't know what was bad and what was good, or whether I was bad or good. I hadn't had sex since Duane. I had no desire for it, and even if I had, I didn't want to be betrayed again. And I didn't want to have to think of myself as a prostitute if I engaged in it, especially if I enjoyed it—which hadn't happened yet. At twenty years old, I was still living with my parents and very confused.

The world saw two devoted parents. Parents who gave their child piano lessons, beautiful clothes, a dog, vacations to Lake Arrowhead or Lake Tahoe in the summer, and a Sweet Sixteen birthday party at the swank Tail O' the Cock. I yearned for someone to see beneath the pretty picture that appeared to be my life, but no one ever did. I ached for a mother who would put her arms around me and tell me the words I longed to hear: "I love you, sweetheart. Darling, what can I do to make it better? *You can talk to me.*"

My folks were very gregarious and had several clusters of friends: the poker group, the travel group, and the business group that sometimes overlapped with the travel group. They were generous, talented, and sometimes funny people, but I could never talk with them honestly, nor could I talk to my friends about what was really going on in my life. Looking back, I can see I was embarrassed and ashamed of the way I was treated and I never allowed myself to speak of it with anyone. My life was, in essence, a sham.

I was forever trying to define my life, but it was impossible. Just about the time that I realized I should expect criticism over everything I did or said, and felt I had a handle on who they were, they would shift. My parents would make an exception, or create a diversion, like a movie, a dinner out, or some other fun activity. *If I could just sort through the confusion,* I'd tell myself, *I'm sure I would feel better.* But how to sort it out? To question them or argue with them was dangerous. They would throw it back at me, mock me, and shame me into agreeing with them.

"There must have been a mistake at the hospital," they'd sometimes say. Could I have been switched at birth? Were my real parents out there somewhere, hoping to find me and give me all their pent-up love?

"She's not much but she's all we've got," my father would say. My parents would laugh about this. It didn't feel like a joke to me.

I developed a compulsion for sweets, taking comfort in food. As a result, my weight would often balloon by ten pounds. Even though I'd tell my mother I'd decided to go on a diet, she would continue to make high caloric dinners. Whenever I resisted her homemade desserts, a look of disappointment would cross her face.

"Just this one day is okay. It's what you eat every day that counts."

Rather than hurt her feelings, I ate it.

The next day I would resume my attempt to diet. But the pattern would start all over again. Fattening food. The look of disappointment if I didn't have two helpings and vigorously compliment her on her cooking. On occasion I'd summon my courage again. I'd announce my intent to diet, and hold my breath anticipating whatever new guilt trip would await me.

～

My father could be affectionate and fun to be around. Sometimes, when preparing for a barbeque party, he'd put on some Broadway show tunes, and we'd sing and dance together around the pool. But I could never count on it. The very next day he could just as soon bellow, "You never gave us a moment's happiness."

On rare occasions, I let them know their words hurt me.

"We're not going to watch our words. We're not going to walk on eggshells."

There were so many things I wanted to say, but unlike them, I *did* have to watch my words so I said nothing. I was working, but there was no possibility of my moving out. It would have been considered blasphemy. The only way out that was acceptable to my parents was to marry, as two of my girlfriends had done. There was simply no question of any other future. Until I found "Mr. Right" I was trapped.

Rod – 2012

After exchanging several emails, I introduced Rod to my favorite porn dialogue.

"How would you like to pretend there's another woman who will come join us?"

"I would," he wrote.

"Do you want the head of your cock inside her pussy?"

"Yes."

"That'll feel good?" I asked.

"Yeah, baby."

"I'll tell her to come in and fuck you, slide her pussy all the way down your cock and all the way back up. While she's doing that, I'll be down here licking your nuts, tasting her pussy juice as it comes out of her wet cunt all over your cock as you fuck her."

"Oh God," he said.

"Does that pussy feel tight and good?" I asked.

"Yeah, baby," he wrote.

"You want to fuck that pussy some more?"

"Oh, yes."

"Would you like to get her doggy style and fuck that cunt?"

"Oh, yeah."

"Now it's my turn to fuck you. Do you want the head of your cock inside my wet pussy? I'm gonna slide my cunt all the way down your dick. I'm going to fuck you good. I'm going to ride your fucking cock. I'm going to make you cum all over my face."

"I'm ready."

"Ouuuu yeah, give me your fuckin' load. I want it really bad. I've got my mouth open. I want to catch it all. You getting ready to cum, baby? C'mon, baby, give me all that cum."

He wrote that he came hard and thanked me effusively.

I have since been asked if I believe these men are really coming or if I think they just like the naughty chat. I believe they were really coming. In fact, I have no doubt about it. Why? Because even if I didn't reach orgasm, I can attest that my own arousal during these encounters was real.

Rod asked me if we could talk on the phone. I was tempted but I told him I'd rather keep our communications to online chats. With online chatting I could maintain some distance. Still, it intrigued me. I wondered what his voice would sound like. I wondered if he'd be as sexy. I wondered what phone sex would be like. I had never done that before. What would I say? I wanted to take that next step, but I didn't feel ready and I didn't know if I ever would.

~

From my limited experience on those sites, I didn't think men were getting the kind of excitement they needed in the bedroom, and in my next relationship with a man, I wanted to be sure to supply it. I enjoyed exciting and pleasing a man.

Craig – 2012

Referencing the picture I posted with my hat pulled down over my eyes, Craig wrote,

"Your caution is understandable. I am being cautious too, so I can't fault you. I don't know how to get to know someone through emails though, so ... next time I'm in Venice I'll search out the hat and we'll have our chance encounter that way."

Craig wanted to meet me and I declined.

"Why?"

"I doubt I'll ever meet anyone in person from this site." I explained to him that I thought it was unseemly because it was a sex site. That was partly the reason; the other part was that I had lied about my age.

"I'll meet you for a drink, a place of your choice," he said. "You can pick a conspicuous spot if you prefer, like a park bench on a lawn near you, so you can drive by and run away if I turn out to be awful, or you can introduce yourself if I'm not. What do you say?"

I wanted to say yes.

Our chat was filled with clever repartee. He was not interested in having naughty chat with me, but in getting to know me as a person. He thought naughty chat was dumb and he needed visual clues, or taste or scent. I kept trying to think of some way to meet this man.

"Are you disappointed we're not having naughty chat?"

"Not at all," I said.

I loved talking about whatever came to our minds. He spoke of the cat he fed that would come to visit, but not to stay, and about the nervy raccoons who liked the cat's food and were prepared to fight over it. He wanted to know what led me to the site—whether it was an accident or on purpose.

"Actually, what I'd really like to know is how did you even get that photo? Were you hiding out from paparazzi?"

I loved our banter. And afterward I felt deeply disappointed. Just imagine: This guy thought I didn't want to meet him, when in fact, I felt just the opposite. Had I hurt his feelings by rejecting his invitation to meet?

It never occurred to me that Craig might also have lied about his age.

~

I spoke to my therapist about Craig, how I'd like to have met him, how disappointed I felt that I couldn't. My therapist said he was mystified by my thinking when I told him I felt an element of respect, regard, and interest from the men on these sex sites.

"This is a fantasy life, and the people on these sites have zero feelings."

But I was on these sites, and I had feelings, even though I did know they were evoked by a fantasy.

On My Way – 1962

Life changed for the better in the summer of my twentieth year. I planned a trip to Europe and saved my salary from working as a secretary for a talent agency in Beverly Hills. My parents agreed to pay for half the trip, which was a very generous act. I traveled alone until I landed in England, where I met up with a tour called "American Youth Abroad." Looking back, given how controlling my parents were, I am amazed they let me go. The truth is, I never knew how it was going to be with them. They could be great, normal, generous, and fun, or they could pull the rug out from underneath me with heartbreaking cruelty. This time I got lucky.

I left Los Angeles International Airport and stopped in New York to see some relatives before embarking on a cruise ship, the *SS France*, to London. I will remember that trip until the day I die.

My cousins, Charles and Maggie, took me to Jones

Beach to see the film *Around the World in 80 Days* and we also visited a very lovely restaurant. While I had been accustomed to eating in nice restaurants, I had never seen such a large number of plates and silverware before me. Courses of scrumptious food were presented, a feast for the eyes as well as the stomach. The service, silverware, food, and view have come back to me in memories many times throughout my life..

I also spent time in New York with another cousin, Lena, and her husband Art. They escorted me to my ship the morning I set sail for London. Lena hugged me every time we saw each other, and all my cousins embraced me with love and warmth. I was slow to hug back. I wasn't used to people, especially blood relations, being so nice to me. Feeling awkward in my own skin, it took me time to return affection, or to trust it. But it grew on me and I liked it. My father had tried many times to convince me of my mother's love, mentioning off-handedly that she just wasn't affectionate, as if this was insignificant. But after experiencing Lena's hugs and smiles, I thought it was very significant.

Lena gave me my first full-length dress. It was a sleeveless black sheath with a square neck and it fit me to perfection. I was thrilled to have such a grown-up dress. With a pretty face and figure, I made a striking appearance.

We visited six countries: Great Britain, Italy, Germany, Switzerland, France, and Liechtenstein. I had a boyfriend in each one except for Liechtenstein. But I didn't have sex with any of them. The experience with

Duane wasn't far from my mind.

By the time our tour bus arrived in Paris, our last stop, I was out of money. I wired home but the wire came back, "Moved." My parents moved? I laughed about this. Of course my parents didn't move. I shrugged it off and used my last few francs to buy myself a hamburger at a local coffee house. That's where I met Michel.

I probably could have lived out a luxurious life in Paris had I been interested in Michel, a rich French bachelor. He was very gallant. He whisked me away to the *Folies Bergère* and a day-long trip outside of Paris. He genuinely liked me, but I was still crazy about Sergio, the Italian singer I'd met the week before in a café in Florence.

I never saw either Sergio or Michel again, but we wrote for some time, and experiences with both are sealed and seared in my memory. They reside there alongside memories of Anthony, the young priest in the Vatican who escorted me to the church bar for drinks. Yes, the Vatican has a bar where you can get any kind of liquor you want.

A few days later, I received a money wire from my parents. I knew they hadn't moved!

∾

It was close to midnight when I arrived back at LAX. My parents and Nana picked me up at the airport, and an hour later we were back in The Valley. Exhausted from the trip, I looked forward to getting home to our apartment and into bed. I also wanted some moments by myself to recapture memories of the trip before the reality of my return set in.

"I want to show you a house I decorated," my father told me.

"Now?"

"It'll only take a minute," he answered.

This was the last thing I wanted to do, but it seemed to mean a lot to him, and I felt I had no choice, so I said okay. We arrived at the home, but it wasn't really a design job, it was our new house that they had purchased while I was in Europe. Now I understood why that wire came back to me.

I couldn't think straight from all of the time zones I'd crossed, but my parents expected compliments, which I gave them as best I could in my jet-lagged state of mind. I told them what a wonderful job they'd done with the house, though I was not truly able to appreciate it at that moment.

The next day I unpacked my suitcase and showed my mother the dress Lena had given me, wanting to share my excitement with her.

"The dress is not appropriate and Lena should not have bought it for you."

After having been gone six weeks, I had forgotten for a moment what it was like at home; how my happiness could so easily become an invitation for my mother to insult, degrade, and undermine me, or someone I cared about, someone who had showed me kindness. I tucked the dress away in the back of the closet, knowing I would never have the courage to wear it again.

As a possible consequence of my mother's criticism over the dress, I came to hate their new house. I hated the layout and hated being back under my parent's domination. A part of me had changed irreversibly after having been to Europe. I had a window into another way of living. My view of life was larger. I'd been introduced to wine, beer, and gaiety, and for once it had been fun just being alive. I knew I wanted more from life than my parents and their houses. And I had to make it happen. Somehow.

But in the meantime, I had to survive living with them. Following my trip to Europe, and all the joy I experienced, I found living at home oppressive. I felt buried under constant criticism and negativity. I felt that therapy could help me but I had no money. I found a job as a secretary, but I wasn't making enough to pay for it. A co-worker told me about a psychologist she liked. I knew my parents didn't think highly of psychologists and realized the only chance I'd have at getting help was to carefully plan how I would approach them. It came together one afternoon when my mother and I were home alone.

"A girlfriend at work and her boyfriend are going away together for the weekend," I said.

"And I suppose you think that's okay?"

"I do."

At this point in the early sixties, you were thought a loose woman if you went away with a boy without the marriage seal of approval, and I anticipated my comment might elicit the response from my mother that it did.

"If you think that then you need a psychiatrist," she said.

"Yes, I think I do."

This time I got what I wanted: the hoped-for blessing from my parents to get therapy.

Moving Out – 1963

I didn't tell my parents beforehand that I was moving
out. I knew they would try to stop me and I didn't feel
strong enough to combat them.

Therapy was helping to some degree. All the wires
that were crossed in my head couldn't be uncrossed in a
short period of time, but by virtue of the fact that I was now
looking for a place to live, I believed I was making
progress.

I located the ideal apartment in Brentwood. It was on
the other side of the hill from The Valley, which gave me
some distance from my parents. It had a beautiful
swimming pool, lush grounds, and a market nearby. On
one of my visits I met a man who agreed to help me move.
All I owned were my clothes, some makeup, and a hair
dryer, so there wasn't much to transport. I couldn't afford
the apartment by myself, so I needed to find a roommate. I
found a woman my age, twenty-one, who was fun to be

with, but more importantly, she was a stewardess who would be away most of the time. The idea of having my own apartment was a momentous event in my life. Along with therapy, I was certain my trip to Europe had some influence over my decision for independence. In fact, I moved out on July 4, Independence Day, a symbolic statement I was very proud of.

Decades later, my father told me that up until the time I left home, everything was fine. He thought everything was fine? *What have you done to your mind, to your soul, that you could have thought everything was fine?*

The Perfect Dress – 1963

My mother and father built their second and final home
on a cul-de-sac nestled in between two houses which were
under construction on Caribeth Drive in Encino. By now
they were accomplished designers. The living room, den,
and bedrooms had floor-to-ceiling windows and looked out
to the pool and beyond, to the expanse of the San Fernando
Valley. The furniture, in burnished oranges and browns,
was high-end yet comfortable. Once the house was in
shape they sent out invitations for a housewarming party.

I had been on my own for a few years at this point. I
wasn't making a lot of money, but knowing this was a
special occasion, I had managed to set a good chunk of a
paycheck aside and headed to Saks Fifth Avenue to find a
stylish and classy dress for this evening. It didn't take me
long to find it. It was black and sexy, but not too revealing.
My shoulders and arms were bare except for thin straps.
There was a small cut-out, diamond-shape, in the midriff

beneath my breasts. I had found the perfect dress.

I drove up to the house on the day of the party and gave the valet my car. As the tall entry doors opened I heard music from a live trio which was strolling through the house. A professional photographer snapped my picture, and two female servers swerved to avoid a collision with the roaming violinist as they passed around hors d'oeuvres. At one end of the living room a bartender mixed drinks. My mother, having prepared all the food herself—rumaki (chicken liver with water chestnut wrapped in bacon), small pizza wedges, lox on toast with caviar—watched proudly as guests ate heartily. Platters of rare roast beef, corned beef, and turkey were displayed on silver trays on the elongated, custom-made dining room table, and the aromas from a variety of desserts, beginning with mother's homemade pecan rolls, wafted from the kitchen. As I looked around, I realized once again: my parents knew how to throw a party.

A few minutes passed before my mother and I caught up to each other. She took one look at me and said coldly, "That dress is inappropriate." I was overcome. I had made such an effort to find something that would suit the occasion perfectly and be a little sexy at the same time. My mother didn't dress conservatively, but she dressed with class. That's what I tried to emulate, with a little extra panache to express my personality. It was always the little extra panache that grated on her. I think if she could have sucked the sensuality right out of me she would have.

But, as in childhood, her words and disapproval had an

impact on me. I spent the rest of the party hiding behind doorways or in the kitchen with the help where I wouldn't be seen, reluctant to talk to anyone.

The next day, my mother called and asked me to go with her to see an apartment building she and my father were thinking about buying. I drove out to The Valley and picked her up. We were in one of the empty apartments alone.

"You looked like a tramp last night," she said.

And for the first time in my life I reacted with true anger.

"Fuck you," I said.

She slapped my face hard.

In that instant I realized I wasn't a child, and that I didn't have to take it. I slapped her back.

∾

I did not feel good about what I had done. It was agonizing for me that my mother and I were at such odds with one another. It was early evening when I received a call from my father.

"If you ever do anything like that again, I'll disown you."

I didn't eat. I didn't sleep. I just replayed the incident in my head over and over, locked in a futile battle to force the outcome to be different. But, of course, it never was.

~

I did not bounce back easily from one of these episodes. I had moved out, but I was not free. No matter how hard I tried to break my emotional bonds with my parents, a large part of me still remained tethered to them.

Many years later I learned that a classic reaction to child abuse is intense attachment to the abusers. The conflict of wanting to stay away and wanting to be close haunted me until their deaths.

NEAR MISS – CIRCA—2012

A Short Story

I only needed a few things. This wouldn't be my once-a-week marathon shopping ordeal where I'd pick up Ketel One vodka for Stuart, banana-pineapple popsicles for Zoey, and a couple of dozen other items. I estimated it would take me fifteen minutes at most. That left me with two hours to myself to get a manicure, massage, or simply luxuriate in a long bath before my family would return home.

I felt him before I saw him. Hurriedly, I rounded the corner from the vegetable section to the dairy display and ran smack into him. His hands, gentle and warm, took hold of my arms to soften the impact. A second later, I would have missed him.

"Oh, I'm sorry!" I said.

"No, it's my fault," he graciously responded.

When my eyes focused on his face, I barely breathed. I had an instant desire for this man, a man I did not know and would probably never see again. He could have stepped right out of a movie: tall, broad-shouldered, hair graying at the temples, but it wasn't just his looks. His scent was a mixture of citrus and something indefinable, but erotic, and his voice was inviting and reassuring.

"Are you hurt?" he asked.

"Oh, no, are you?"

He laughed. "I'm fine. Listen, that was...I'm a big guy...you could have been hurt."

"But I wasn't."

There was something in the way he floundered that made him even more attractive.

"I don't know," he added, "I don't do well with head-on collisions. I could use a drink. What about you?"

I knew I should have said *I have to get home to my husband and child.* I had the words formed but they never came out.

～

We had drinks at a small bar nearby, somewhere I'd never been. It wasn't fancy, and it wasn't busy.

We gravitated to a booth in the back. A moment ago, I was a faithful wife. Now I was exploring the forbidden, which both set me on edge and excited me. Before we arrived, I worried about seeing someone I knew, but when we entered, I became more relaxed. My friends and family went more for the high rent district.

From the confident way he carried himself, and that off-kilter smile of his, I knew he'd be a good lover. I fantasized about his mouth on my clit as I, oh so ladylike, sipped my Mojito. I found myself wishing we weren't making small talk and were instead making love.

"I'm married," I blurted out.

He laughed. "So that's what that ring on your finger means!"

I could feel my face flush. How silly of me not to realize that of course he would have noticed my ring.

"I don't care if you don't care," he whispered.

I took my commitment to my marriage seriously, but at that moment, I *didn't* care. I'd had a moment of sanity and then it left me. It had been more than two months since Stuart and I had sex, and even then it wasn't very good. Eight years of marriage had dulled our sex life. Or that's what I told myself. I suspected an affair was more probably the reason. Stuart had a very attractive female partner in his architectural firm. She had been "Miss America" or

"Miss California" or Miss Something or Other. I brought it up once and he denied any involvement with her. But in addition to no sex, there had been a disconnect lately, and I felt he had lost interest in our relationship.

"Are you married?" I asked.

"No."

He must have caught the look on my face.

"Would you prefer that I were?"

"No. I was just feeling a little envious. You have nothing to hide."

"Everyone has something to hide. My name is David, by the way."

David. David and Goliath. Strong name.

"Kate."

He took my hand and kissed my palm. Then he sucked on a finger. From that, I knew I would orgasm with him.

~

I let David sign us in the motel. The room was passable, not where I wanted to be with him, but we couldn't go to an upscale hotel. Too big a chance of being seen.

He kissed me. Enveloped me. I had experienced a million kisses, but none were as sensual or passionate as his. He had one arm on the small of my back, pulling me in. The other was holding my head as he kissed me deeper, making me his even before taking me.

It wasn't the size of his cock so much as what he did with it, the sensations he created by angling it to press on my g-spot, for instance. It had been so long since I had sex like this; slow, deliberate movements to give me maximum pleasure.

Somewhere in the middle of my euphoria, I wondered how I would deal with it if this were just a one-time occurrence. We weren't even through and I wanted more of it, more of him.

I came many times. He told me afterward, "I love to watch you cum." I wanted to cum again for him, over and over.

I glanced at the clock by the bedside. My husband was picking up my daughter from school, and they would be home soon.

"I have to go," I said, reluctantly.

"Will I see you again?" he asked.

How I wanted to say *yes, you will see me every day, every minute, every second that you're available.* But I had a husband, and even though I questioned the state of our marriage, I still loved him. And I didn't know for sure that Stuart was having an affair. But I knew I was. And as much as I wanted it, craved it, desired it, I couldn't continue with David. I knew it would tear me apart. A chance meeting was one thing. An ongoing relationship was another.

"I guess your silence means no."

I couldn't speak. I just nodded.

"I won't forget you, you know," he said.

My eyes watered.

~

I've thought of David many times over the years, wondering if I did the right thing. Three years later Stuart and I divorced. It became obvious to both of us that our connection had waned, and though we tried, it just couldn't be resuscitated.

I still live in the same neighborhood, still shop at the same market. I'd hoped to have another near miss and run into David again, but I never did. I've wondered if he moved or never even lived in the local area to begin with. The yearning is still there for him, and with it, a feeling of loss, even regret at having left him in that run-down room without any way to contact me. But though I know the memory of our lovemaking will stay with me forever, I also know our moments together were something to be grateful for. I can live with that.

Morton – 1964

I took a job as a secretary with Paramount Studios.
My boss was a film producer looking for investors. A man
named Morton came into the office one afternoon to
discuss being one of them. Morton was literally a genius
who worked at Caltech as a professor. He also had an
interest in me. I didn't want to become involved with a
married man, but my resolve to avoid it was not very
strong. He invited me out for a drink, which turned into
dinner, which turned into a plane ride some dates later, with
Morton piloting us to San Diego.

Sex with Norton was disappointing. He did not show
an interest in oral sex and he came soon after he entered
me. But I was utterly taken with Morton's mind and sense
of humor, and had an intense sexual attraction regardless. I
would wait for his calls, which came only occasionally. I
fantasized about him relentlessly. Three months into my
fixation, Morton told me that he, along with his wife and

three children, were moving to Bozeman, Montana for him to teach there. How could this be possible? How would I ever see him again? Food lost its taste, and sleep came in fits and starts.

I had switched jobs again during the course of my knowing Morton. At my new position at a literary agency, I got friendly with a client. His name was Nigel and he lived in Tacoma, Washington. He had driven to Los Angeles for business and was headed back after his meeting at the agency.

I searched my brain for a way to see Morton again. I asked Nigel if I could ride with him until he got near home, and then I would take a Greyhound Bus the rest of the way...to Montana. Nigel was married and I wasn't interested in him; this was simply an adventure I wanted to have. He said yes. I knew there was never any danger that Nigel would treat me other than respectfully.

I was not due any vacation time yet at my new job so I gave notice, and soon I was on the road heading north with Nigel. The trip was uneventful, and when I arrived in Washington, I boarded a bus for Montana. I was on my way to see my married lover, though he had no idea I was coming.

It wasn't difficult to find a hotel in Bozeman, Montana. In fact, it wasn't hard to find anything. It was a small town, and wherever you wanted to go was within walking distance. I went up to my room and called the operator. Morton's phone number and address were listed. I decided to go there that very afternoon. At 3:00 p.m. on a crisp fall day, I knocked on the door of my married lover's home. A boy of about six answered the door. It never occurred to me to ask myself what I would have said or done if his wife had been the one to greet me.

Morton was home. He didn't seem that surprised to see me, but he must have been. He had spoken often about his two-year-old son, Ari, and I asked to see him. Morton instructed me to wait for him at the end of the block. A few minutes later he came out carrying his son.

"I came from L.A. to see you," I said.

"This is Ari," he said, perhaps not knowing how to respond to my statement.

We spoke for a few minutes, and he invited me to lunch the next day at the university. It wasn't anything he said, but the way he said it, that told me this was not going to go the way I had hoped. Morton was not going to leave his wife for me.

The next day we met at the college cafeteria. I was very uncomfortable throughout that lunch because he asked me nothing personal and offered nothing personal. Small talk, that's all it was. He didn't suggest a relationship in the future for us, or even say if he ever thought of me. He was just...*polite.* I'd rather have died than have him treat me politely. When we parted he wished me good luck. *Good luck!* I had a good cry that night.

A New Start - 1964

The day after my disastrous reunion with Morton, I boarded the bus again, this time heading back to Los Angeles. The bus made a stop for lunch in Sun Valley, Idaho. You'd think I would have given up on the idea of a future with Morton, but I didn't. That's how powerful my fantasy life was, and the distorted belief that somewhere inside him he cared for me.

Sun Valley is known for its great skiing, so I thought it might be fun to work there in the winter, and if per chance Morton should change his mind, well, it wouldn't be a long flight from Bozeman to Sun Valley. I knew the chance of that happening was remote, but I didn't give up.

I applied for jobs as a maid, but it was August and all of the domestic jobs were taken already, which was a good thing because I would have been a horrible maid. I didn't have a good attitude for it. But I couldn't think of anything else I could do.

The bus was waiting. I noticed a coffee shop in front of it. I entered and heard someone playing the piano in an adjoining room, which turned out to be a bar. I popped my head in and saw an elderly man who played appalling piano.

"May I speak to the manager of the coffee shop?" I asked a busboy. I was thinking maybe I could be a waitress, though again, I would have been as good a waitress as I would have a maid. He pointed me to a middle-aged woman.

"Hi, are you the manager?" I asked.

"I'm the owner," she said. "Can I help you?"

"I'm looking for work in the winter."

"What do you do?"

Somewhere in between the bar and the coffee shop this thought must have penetrated my brain: *I could do better than that*, because suddenly I heard myself say, "I play the piano."

She smiled brightly. "We're looking to open a bar on the other side of this coffee shop, and we're going to need a piano player."

"If you send me my train fare, I'll come back in the fall," I said brazenly. My piano lessons as a teenager were of no use to me now. I had forgotten nearly everything I knew. Had she asked me to audition, I couldn't have played a thing. Luckily, she didn't.

I had yearned for a life away from secretarial work, one where I was challenged creatively and one that would bring some excitement into my life. Maybe this was it!

I returned to Los Angeles and waited to see if she'd send me the train fare. She did! I was to begin performing in two weeks. Only after I received the money wire did I call my old piano teacher, Henry Pfeiffer, to set up a lesson. Henry was not only an accomplished teacher, but a fine jazz musician. He taught at his house in West Hollywood. Henry had five pianos: two side-by-side black grand pianos in his front studio (one was his, not to be touched by anyone but him), an upright piano in each of his two middle studios, and one out back in his converted garage.

"Play something for me," he said.

To give myself the best chance, I used sheet music rather than try to rely on memory. I selected a simple piece and began to play.

"Stop!" he said emphatically, before I was halfway through.

I instantly removed my hands from the keyboard and said nothing. This was not a good sign.

"You'll have to start over from day one as if you never had a lesson."

"But I have to start performing in two weeks!" I said. This was not at all what I'd bargained for.

"I don't care," Henry said.

If I wanted to study with Henry I had no choice. I knew one thing for sure: I had to live and breathe music. I remembered when, as a teenager, I had taken one lesson a week from him and had found that arduous. Now I was barreling through three lessons a day and practicing sixteen hours a day! I lived and breathed music. Could I keep up the pace? Could I even remember what I'd learned? Scales, chords, minor 7ths, 10ths, stretching my hands to reach a span of ten notes for a fuller, richer sound and almost making it. As soon as I mastered one lesson, we moved on to the next. The feel of the keys beneath my fingers was intoxicating.

As the days and the lessons multiplied, Henry shook his head in admiration. "I've never seen anybody do this before."

I resented having to take the time to eat and sleep, and they became incidental in my life. All that mattered was conquering the challenge ahead of me. Henry offered me his garage piano on which to practice. When I finished my eight hours at Henry's, I drove to UCLA, praying there'd be a music room available. Going back to my apartment was not an option. No neighbor was going to tolerate my practicing eight hours every day. After UCLA, when I finally returned home to my tiny single that barely had room for a rental piano, I practiced another four hours. I was worried my neighbors would complain, but they told me they enjoyed it!

Finally, when I was ready, Henry allowed me to graduate to a real song. I bought "cheat sheet" books from him which were collections of popular music, and he started me off on standards from the thirties and forties: "More Than You Know," "It Had to be You," and "I'll Be Seeing You." When I learned those, he'd acquiesce to a current song or two.

Additionally, I needed to learn how to sing. But I

couldn't find a singing coach. I asked Henry, but he didn't know anyone. I would have to teach myself. Henry suggested I sing the scales so at least I'd be on key, so that's what I did. Nobody ever told me you're not supposed to sing and play the melody; it's one or the other, but I didn't know that.

I invested one hundred and ten percent of my intellect and energies in my music. It was glorious! I had never felt a greater purpose to my life. But what made me think I could become a professional musician in two weeks? Youth? Arrogance? Probably both, but once I made the commitment in my head, nothing was going to stop me. All that mattered was meeting this important deadline. No thoughts of sex or men even entered my mind.

I was learning something fun that challenged me and I loved it, and somehow, some way, at the end of two weeks, I had enough songs under my belt to dare to pronounce myself to the world a professional pianist. I'd have to fake the rest.

Henry drove me to the train station downtown and waited while I bought my ticket for the trip to Sun Valley, Idaho. Then he wished me good luck. On the five-day train ride I didn't gaze out the window at the passing scenery. I studied my cheat sheets and played an invisible piano.

Two days after arriving I began my job as a pianist/vocalist. Not a secretary anymore!

Sun Valley, Idaho – 1964

The room I rented above the small house was sparse and didn't even have a bathroom. I had to go downstairs in the home to use it, but I didn't care. I was thrilled to be there.

In long, pretty dresses and heels every night, I dressed the part of a glamorous nightclub performer. And I sang and played my heart out. I had been in a straightjacket as a secretary, discouraged from talking, let alone socializing, with clients. Now, at a piano bar, I'd been hired for the *purpose* of being friendly, with a little music thrown in.

My anxiety level was high. I was going to be center stage and after only two weeks of lessons. I could have loosened up by having a drink at work as many were bought for me, but I wasn't sure I could function at a high level with alcohol in my system and I didn't want to take the chance. Requests for a wide variety of songs were called out to me, and I did my best to fill them. A week later I was fired.

Since I hadn't been able to take singing lessons I was certain my voice was the problem. Years later, when recalling this time in my life, I realized my firing had more to do with my not being able to relate to the locals rather than the quality of my voice. The young people my age who came to ski didn't hang out there, and the patrons who did were decades older than me. I just didn't fit in.

So what does a nice Jewish girl do while trying to figure out her next move? She goes to the nearest beauty salon! I went to get my hair done at Sun Valley Lodge and told my stylist my tale of woe. If I didn't get another job I knew any chance to see Morton again, if in fact he decided to come see me, would vanish. I had just sent him a letter the day before, letting him know my whereabouts.

"I think Warm Springs Ranch Inn may be looking for some entertainment," she said.

The restaurant was a beautiful lodge-inspired structure overlooking the Warm Springs Creek. Hemingway used to hang out there, I was told.

"Looking for any entertainment for the winter?" I asked the manager.

"What do you do?"

"This time with conviction I said, "I play the piano." Believing my voice had been my downfall at my previous gig, I wasn't about to tell him I sang.

"We're thinking of getting a piano."

And my new job was born. I performed every afternoon from five to nine except Sunday. That was the day the skiers went home and the next wave of guests arrived for the week. This was the right environment for me. I met people near my age, and they were consistently a classy group. There was often applause at the end of each number. I basked in the audience's acceptance of me.

I felt sexy in nightclub attire and knew I looked good. Between the ski vacationers and the ski instructors, you'd think I would have met someone there, but it just didn't happen. My sexual desire was wrapped up in Morton, and whether I realized it or not at the time, I think I signaled that I was unavailable so I was rarely approached.

Meanwhile, I had to look for another place to live. I was being evicted. A relative was coming to visit, and they needed the room. I found a small apartment with a bath. With a bath! I could pee anytime I wanted! The first night I got back about ten o'clock, ready to get a good night's sleep. Only one problem: there was no heat. No heat in the winter in Sun Valley, Idaho, where the temperature dipped below freezing at night. And there was no one to call at that hour to get it fixed.

There was hot water in the shower, so I turned it on, thinking the steam from it would drift out into the bedroom and keep me warm. I tried to sleep but couldn't. The noise from the running water and the frigid conditions kept me awake. There was only one thing to do if I wanted to survive, somehow get up to the Sun Valley lodge.

To stave off the cold I dressed quickly: long underwear, ski pants, turtleneck T-shirt, pullover sweater, down parka, woolen scarf. Then I grabbed my gloves and took off on foot. The temperature was falling fast. I had never been so cold in all my life. It was late by ski resort standards, nearly eleven o'clock, by the time I reached the main road which led to the Sun Valley Lodge. There was no traffic, which meant no ride, which meant I would have to walk all the way if I lived that long.

Who am I kidding? Skiers go to bed early so they can rise early to ski on fresh snow. I'll be lucky to see even one car on this road. I knew that I might not make it up to the lodge before freezing to death, but I had to risk it. I had no other choice. Either face certain death in my room or take my chances on the road.

Five minutes passed, then seven, then eight and no cars. Then I stopped checking my watch. I walked as fast as I could, but you don't move fast in ski gear. *Oh God, please send me a car.* In Los Angeles, I'd never hitch a ride with a stranger, but here I knew I was safe. Then it started to snow. The temperature might rise a few degrees, but now no one would see me if they did come by.

I thought I heard a car. I turned around and saw headlights. I stepped off the curb onto the road and waved frantically. The car stopped and I climbed in, thanking the driver profusely for picking me up.

I arrived at the Sun Valley Lodge a few minutes later and zeroed in on a sofa. Just as I was about to close my eyes, I felt a tap on my shoulder. The management, it seemed, didn't much care for my sleeping arrangement; but instead of throwing me out, they kindly offered me a room where they put up their employees. The next day my heat was fixed.

Ben's Fantasy - 2012

I logged on to Benaughty.com and there was an IM
(instant message) from Benjamin. We had chatted before
and I lit up when I saw his moniker, *Imsexyforyou.*

His message read: "I was fantasizing about you today."

"Really? What was your fantasy?" I wrote.

"I was daydreaming that you invited me back to your
apartment. You offered me a glass of wine. After we had a
glass of wine, you led me to your bed. We began to kiss
and you unzipped my jeans."

I pictured him in low-riders, shirt off, revealing a
sculptured chest. "Go on."

"You pulled my boxers down and started stroking my
hard cock."

In my mind, I saw a deliciously erect member of
significant girth.

"Then what?" I asked, with great curiosity.

"My cock was pulsing, precum dripping."

"And then?"

"You gave me the best hand job I ever had in my life. Came like a fire hose."

"Wow." Now I didn't even have to be online to bring a man to orgasm!

"Since you gave me pleasure," he added, "I'd like to give you some."

"What did you have in mind?" I asked, my senses heightened.

Our conversation moved to oral sex, both of us acknowledging that we enjoyed that aspect of lovemaking.

"I would love to go down on you and make you cum over and over again. Will you let me? Can we meet?"

The warning lights flashed brightly. "I don't think so."

"Why not?" he wrote.

"I'm not looking to meet anyone on this site."

"Why not?" he asked.

I explained my reservations, that it seemed unseemly, which didn't make all that much sense since I was having erotic phone chat with him, a virtual stranger. But that's how I felt at the time. And I'd have to confess my true age, not an insignificant detail.

"Just so you know," he added, "I'm going to try and persuade you. I want to hold you and kiss you. I want to slowly undress you. I want to look into your eyes as I cum inside you."

Later, I did think about meeting him. It was impossible not to.

Becoming Me - 1964

Making music filled me with happiness. I had always loved singing show tunes at home and now it was my occupation! The customers at Warm Springs Ranch Inn liked me and told their fellow travelers about me. Business was flourishing in the bar, but I was aimless during the day. I had written Morton at the university, but received no reply. I didn't know if I ever would. My days were long and I was aware of needing a purpose.

The last thing I wanted was to learn how to ski. Never athletic, I had taken a lesson on the bunny slope in the California mountains and had not done well. Not grasping the idea of how to stop myself, I had almost catapulted over the edge. I wasn't eager to repeat that experience.

Everyone came up there to ski but me. I decided if I was going to remain in Sun Valley I would have to buck up and try again. I didn't look forward to it, but like the multitude of endeavors I faced throughout my life that I didn't want to do, I shored up the courage and did it anyway.

Gradually, with lessons, I gained some measure of confidence. One morning I took myself to the line leading to the chairlift to ski down my first real slope. The chairlift itself was an exercise in courage. Having no one to ski with, I decided to ski alone. Bad idea. After exiting the chairlift, I found myself on a catwalk. It was very narrow (maybe that's why they're called catwalks; only a cat could manage it) and it was a sheer drop to the bottom of the mountain. I inched my way along. There was no fluidity to my movements, only one heart-stopping, clunky step after another. Suddenly, one of my skis came off and flew down the mountain.

Panic set in. The thoughts that came to my mind in rapid succession were: *How am I going to get down to the bottom now? I hope no one gets killed by that menace of a ski.*

I told myself that someone had to come by, but having skied alone was a risk. There was no guarantee I would ever come across another human being, and no one appeared.

A shadow crept over the mountain and the temperature was dipping fast. I soon surmised that the only hope I had of getting down the mountain was to sit on my butt and scoot all the way down. And that is what I did.

When I finally made it to the base of the mountain two hours later, I took myself to one of the local pubs to celebrate the fact that I was alive and uninjured, which was more than the skier who came in after me could do. With a cast up to her thigh, she had to be assisted to a table. Having a cast on your leg couldn't have been fun.

From then on I stuck to the smallest mountain, and each time I secured myself on the chairlift I'd look skyward and say, "God, if you just get me down this mountain I promise I'll never do it again." The next day I would go up and speak to God again.

He or She was a merciful God and never said to me: "What's with you? You make the same promise to me every day. One of these days I'm going to stop listening." But each time I got down the mountain safely.

Working and living in Sun Valley was a great experience, and a major accomplishment. I proved to myself that I could set a goal and accomplish it, and that I could be creative and make a living at it. But after two months I was growing weary of making new friends at the beginning of the week and saying good-bye to them at the end. I knew I'd never see any of them again. The feeling of loss was starting to take a toll. And I finally recognized that Morton wasn't going to come see me. I realized it would be foolish to pursue him any further. I decided to quit my job. The good news was that I had been there six weeks and had not been fired!

The big question was: Could I make my living this way once I returned to Los Angeles?

The Sound of Music – 1965

After I returned to Los Angeles I took three more
weeks of lessons from Henry. I don't remember why I
never went beyond the three weeks. Perhaps it was the
money. Perhaps I knew I had the basics and needed to test
my abilities in the real world.

Although my piano playing skills had only marginally
improved, I still managed somehow to find jobs in Los
Angeles I was constantly scouring the city for auditions.
Sometimes I'd get booked for only a night or two, and
some jobs were in unpopular or out-of-the-way restaurants,
where only one or two couples would show up. But it was
still worthwhile to me. Los Angeles was bursting at the
seams with musicians who sought work on a daily basis, so
finding employment as a paid musician in Los Angeles was
no small achievement.

But I couldn't take all the credit. At least not in terms
of musicianship. I was an attractive, sexy woman, and the

bars wanted businessmen, or any men, who could afford to, and were interested in, spending money. Often, said men spent hours and downed a substantial amount of liquor, and sometimes food, around my piano bar. I must admit I did enjoy looking glamorous and I enjoyed the attention they gave me.

My mother's health began to worsen. My parents weren't going out as much and she knew I needed clothes for work, so she gave me some of her evening dresses. Her clothes were more conservative than the ones I purchased for myself, but they were beautiful and classy, and fit me perfectly. I wore low-cut this and high-slit that, and fortunately I had a pretty face and shapely figure. I could play basic piano, and whether I thought I had a good voice or not, I had to sing. It was the job requirement everywhere I sought work.

Sometimes I was provided with a bass player and drummer. I knew my skills on the piano weren't the caliber of what they were used to, but they were always nice to me, and I was stimulated to play better by performing with other musicians.

Every time a new song came out, I headed for my favorite music store in Hollywood. I became a sheet-music junkie. I revered each piece of music and treasured going over it many times to learn it. Not trusting my mind from early on, I was afraid to rely on memory. So I brought a small red suitcase of sheet music and cheat books to every job. Nobody seemed to mind that I read music.

At the same time, however proud I was to get work as

a musician, I wasn't making a living. So I collected unemployment and used the time I had to write songs. I composed "Here in This Room" with Morton in mind. It was a sad song full of love and loss, but I liked it. I took my one little song to a small recording studio in Hollywood. The musician who ran the studio accompanied me on guitar. For the first time in my life, I heard my voice echoed and amplified. I sounded great! Exhilarated, I took that record and tried to get an important label to sign me up. No one was interested.

I wrote more music and lyrics, creating as many as three songs a day. A former coworker of mine introduced me to Stone Wallace. He had been a well-established record producer with Chess Records in Chicago, and just formed his own company. Stone liked my music and signed me up. He had other artists record my songs as well.

My parents, who objected to nearly all of my choices, didn't seem to mind that I was performing, or that I traveled to far-reaching destinations to do it. My favorite part of performing was not performing as I had stage fright, but working in a recording studio. I loved hearing my voice amplified, and if you made a mistake you could record over it! And with a full orchestra accompanying me to my own songs … well, this was as close to nirvana as I was ever likely to get.

LYNN BROWN

We re-recorded "Here in This Room."

It was here in this room that our love was first born,
It was here in this room that we found happiness,
It is in this room so plain and worn
That I now know real loneliness.
It was here in this room that we came to play.
Like children, we believed in forevermore.

151

It was here in this room that you said good-bye,
Now here in this room nothing's the same as before.
And me, well I get through the hours.
I see each one pass on the clock.
I can't sleep so well anymore
But that I suppose will change someday.
When I walk out of this room for the very last time
When I leave this room so plain and worn
And I leave all the many tears that I've cried
And this little room where my first real love
Was born and died...
Was born and died.

I continued to write songs and occasionally find work. Unemployment got me through those lean times. I didn't ask my parents for financial help and they didn't offer any. A studio apartment without a kitchen was all I could afford. I used a hot plate to cook meals. My existence was bare and simple, and each day revolved around my music.

The lyrics of "The Home Where Love's In Vain" related to my mother and father, but I disguised it as a woman and her husband because I felt it would be more commercial. I was terrified of revealing myself to both my parents and the world in general. You didn't tell the truth in my family, especially if it was critical of my parents.

I sit here and look around
And wonder why I came.
I see familiar faces

Some I even know by name.
A pretty view, a swimming pool
Are all that now remain
But I recall when life lived here
And love was not in vain.
The guy across the table
Pledged love I thought would last.
But now I'm just a photograph
Bringing up the past.
I could have had someone else get my things.
I should have had someone else return the rings.
No, I had to see if there was still a way
For us to rehearse and start a brand new play.
It's not so very long ago
I called this place my home.
But now it's just four walls to me
And a fireplace of stone.
A pretty view, a swimming pool
Are all that now remain
Except for the sting of strangeness I feel
In the home where love's in vain.

The home where love was in vain: that's what it was to me. I wondered if I would ever find a home where love was not in vain, where I would be loved and accepted.

Sex and Chats and the
Whole Damned Thing - 2012

A nice Jewish girl didn't watch porn, have sex chats, engage in phone sex, or suck cock. And for sure didn't use naughty talk, let alone with men she didn't even know!

I had been caught up for so long in a will-I-survive state of mind, and Jerry's will-he-survive battle, and before that a will-my-mother-survive mindset, every decision I'd ever made, big or small, seemed like a life and death battle.

Having been stuck in automatic thinking from an old belief system, I was beginning to be transformed into a free woman, free to engaged in, and relish, sex. With each chat I was becoming freer. The idea that I would enjoy licking a man's cock while watching him watch me, or even think of dressing up in the bedroom for the sole purpose of exciting him, had been unimaginable.

For some women, an open mind or a good lover may be all they need. For me, I needed a full-on break from the thinking that had been so destructive for me, which often included the inability to think for myself, to determine what was best for me, along with shunning sexual pleasure. My fertile imagination could now be used for more than writing.

While I was apprehensive with Dave, my first online sex partner, it didn't take long for me to flow with it, to be spontaneous with my responses to a variety of men, freeing myself to experience down-and-dirty sex. I could hardly wait to get home to get online. I was a sexually desirable woman again and sexually desiring, coalescing two activities that had before now been separate in my life: sex and fun! I was getting to know my body, touching myself in different ways than before, applying pressure at different levels than before, which often led to orgasm. I heard my own voice when I came. I had never before expressed myself out loud.

The sex chats were helping me to evolve into a more open, more flexible, more complete and integrated identity.

Was there a downside in it for me? I didn't think so because I knew if I had the opportunity for a real relationship, I would drop the chats in a minute. Or would I? This was a one-woman free yourself campaign I had embarked on, and I didn't want to relinquish it until I was satisfied that I had taken it to its natural conclusion. I believed I would know when that was.

Benaughty.com – 2012

Generally, I found that the shorter the email, the more intelligent the man. The converse is also true. Here's an example of a longer message I once received:

"Hello, hows you? I was just checking through profiles and I saw your profile and I enjoyed all what you wrote and I want to give this a go. Letting you know you caught my interest. We should start off being best friends as a foundation to start from."

And two additional very long paragraphs later it was finally over.

While I usually gave a man the courtesy of a response on regular online dating sites, I did not always do that on a sex site. If I found a message distasteful or arrogant I didn't answer.

Despite the fact that I was on a sex site, many of the conversations didn't revolve around sex. Nick, from Spokane, Washington spoke about his job and not having a date on a Saturday night. Sometimes our rapport was so good, I missed certain men when they left the site. I then had to force myself to go on to the next one, which both distracted me and cushioned my disappointed feelings. Maybe in spite of myself I *did* have hopes of meeting someone on this site.

My therapist didn't think much of my having hurt feelings. "It's a sex site," he repeated. "People have zero emotions."

I voiced my usual objection: I had emotions and I was on the site.

~

R.C. contacted me again. The moment I saw I had received a request for a chat from him, I was instantly erotically charged.

"I am reaching out for you," he wrote.

"I'm here."

After some chit-chat back and forth, I asked him, "Are you a good kisser?"

"I got high marks in kissing school."

"Nice," I wrote, smiling to myself.

"Higher marks in licking class," he added.

"Very good to know."

We had, as before, another very hot and heavy exchange.

I was glad R.C. came back for more. I was, as he preferred, wanting and wet (but not yet cumming).

After we finished our conversation I went out to do some errands. As I was driving, my mind drifted back to our chat, his sense of humor, and his intensity. I nearly ran a red light. Internet sex was attention grabbing, no doubt about it.

Parts Unknown – 1967

My unemployment was running out and I needed to
make money in a hurry. I found an agent who booked
piano bar performers. She found me work at two of the
more remote places on this earth. The first was Red Deer,
in Alberta, Canada where I performed for two weeks. It is
so small you can drive through it faster than you can smoke
a cigarette, if you smoke, which I did then. The other was
Anchorage, Alaska in the winter.

Who went to Alaska? No one! Especially not in the
winter. Perhaps there was a good reason for this! I thought
it would be a grand adventure. Picturing a vast wilderness,
I was stunned to find the streets of Anchorage barren of
nature and consisting of mostly one-story buildings—the
majority of them bars.

I had heard there were a lot of men in Alaska. This
could have been a fairytale come true if there had been any
men within shouting range. Whatever men lived there,

were out on fishing boats and oil wells, and for months at a time.

The Captain Cook Hotel provided a very nice room for me. It was what is now considered a boutique hotel. It was only four stories tall, and with a view of the sea that was barely visible in winter's twenty-two hours a day of darkness.

The temperature dipped well below freezing during the day, but no matter, I had to get outside the walls of the hotel. There was a proliferation of bars in Anchorage, three to a block, in fact. I think I stopped in every one. Staying warm was the only thing on my mind. I wasn't interested in drinking, but there were plenty of others who were. Maybe it was the cold. Maybe it was the isolation. I experienced both, and they were rough.

For the first time in my life I was making good money and had lost the desire to spend it. There were no clothing stores or boutiques, only a drugstore that carried necessities.

When I wasn't working, I either read or ate. At night after I finished performing, the busboy with whom I'd become friendly, led me inside the hotel kitchen to the fifteen-foot-tall refrigerators. They were a sight to behold with their huge steel doors leading to vast amounts of desirable food. Needing something to make me feel better about my life, I stuffed myself with goodies. I had my music, but I felt so alone. Gaining ten pounds in six weeks made me feel even worse. I hated myself for putting on weight.

Outside of the busboy I had no one to talk to. The only man in sight was an attorney who was very cold to me, and shot deer for food. I actually ate venison one night at his place. I didn't like it and felt bad about it afterward. It seemed shameful to me to kill a deer for any reason, let alone for food.

I wrote "Out There" when I was at my lowest.

I'm out there, on my own little island,
Out there somewhere very far, far away
Out there where no one can hurt me,
And I cannot hurt in return.
I'm out there, with no one beside me
Out there where nobody goes,
Out there with no one to guide me
And I'm free to hide in return.
I'm out there without friend without foe
Out there with no place to go,
Out there with no one to find me
And nothing ahead of me, nothing behind me.
I'm out there where I've traveled before
Out there so lonely and blue
Out there where I travel once more
'Til I can face the world and you again.
More than to give or to receive
I need to live, need to share my needs
You share when you love, love when you share
'Cause somebody cares.
I'm out there, have you ever been there?

Out there, where it's always the same
Out there, where it's even and peaceful
With just a voice from a dream to call your name.
I'm here now, looking to see
If someone other than me
Comes here, feeling despair,
Needing to share, needing to care,
I'm out here, come and find me,
I'm out here, come and find me,
I'm out here, come and find me.

I spent my twenty-fifth birthday in Alaska in the cold and the dark. It was not only my physical surroundings that were unknown; there were parts of me emotionally that I didn't know and wasn't connected to. I asked my father to call me for my birthday and he did, but it didn't make me feel better. Neither did throwing myself into reading. My mind would race from one thought to another and I had trouble concentrating. My spirits were sinking fast, and I needed to get back home to Los Angeles.

Breakdown – 1968

Nobody ever called it a breakdown, not my parents nor any of my therapists. But what do you call it when you can't function in the outside world if not a breakdown?

I had returned to Los Angeles, but was not well. My emotions had started to overwhelm me, and I found myself crying at the slightest provocation. I suffered severe anxiety, although a new psychiatrist was in the picture who did not identify it as anxiety. He said I felt guilty because of the rage I was feeling toward my mother. I was not aware of feeling rage at that time and I didn't think his assessment was true. All it did was serve to further accelerate the out-of-control feelings that were consuming me. I never saw that doctor again.

Unaware of what was happening to me, and still trying to carry on, I made the attempt to perform at the piano and when I was unable to do, I tried to hold down a simple secretarial job. But I couldn't concentrate and lost that job, too. Repetitive warnings that I was unsafe assaulted my mind. Responding to the warnings, I carved out an increasingly narrow vision for my life, constantly adjusting what I could or couldn't do depending upon what the voices in my head were telling me.

I finally found a position at UCLA, preparing bags to hold blood. It didn't require much thinking on my part, which was good, but it was dull, monotonous, and depressing work. Finally, I couldn't even hold down that job. I was beginning to panic and worried I might be overcome and not be able to control my behavior.

One night, in a wrenching state of anxiety, I called my father and asked him to take me to a mental hospital, not knowing where I got the idea. I had never thought about it before. He said he would take me, but asked if I would like to wait to see how I felt in the morning. I told him I couldn't wait.

I checked into a private psychiatric hospital in Van Nuys. I thought my life was over as I knew it. Part of me was relieved. I wouldn't be burdened with decisions anymore, especially since every decision I made seemed to be the wrong one. My mind would be free. But that wasn't the case; my mind never stopped.

The first night there, I awoke, rose from my bed, and terror-stricken, fainted. Afraid I might pass out other places as well, I needed someone to be with me at all times. Given that I entered voluntarily I could leave for short periods if time if I wanted. I wanted to take a walk and get some fresh air, but I was even frightened to cross the street by myself.

During this period, Stone Wallace wanted to record me again. Fortunately, I was able to convince a nurse from the hospital to drive me to my session. I didn't sing very well, but at the time it was still exciting for me to be able to record again. At least part of me was still alive. But I felt strange being in a perfectly normal environment when I was feeling very abnormal.

I had been at the hospital a month when my father came to tell me he could no longer afford to keep me there. I would have to go to a county hospital. I didn't know how that would impact me, but I knew it wouldn't be good. The county and your health should never be used in the same sentence.

Olive View Psychiatric Hospital was located in the far reaches of the San Fernando Valley. It functioned on regimen. Up at six-thirty in the morning, showers and meds by seven, breakfast at seven-thirty, exercise for an hour at eight-thirty, and so on. The nurses proclaimed me normal and asked what I was doing there. That was the question I kept asking myself. I didn't know why I was there. I just knew I didn't belong anywhere else.

I was kept heavily sedated with Thorazine, their drug of choice. It numbed my mind. The lids of my eyes were never more than half open, and all I wanted to do was sleep. But with sleep came unendurable nightmares; so I dreaded the nights and I dreaded the days. The reality that had become my life was too much to bear. Thoughts of suicide entered my mind.

~

"How are you feeling?" asked the psychiatrist.

It had taken a whole week to get an appointment. I had hopes he could help me.

"I'm not doing well," I answered.

"Well, stay on your meds, and keep up your group therapy. You'll get better in time."

"You mean that's it? We're finished?"

He nodded. "I have other patients to see."

I received less than five minutes of therapy once a week. Contrary to his prediction, I did not get better. I never got used to the routine or the environment. Maybe that was the whole idea. Don't become too comfortable. Maybe you'll be motivated to leave. If that was their goal, it didn't work for me. I was frightened to stay and frightened to leave.

One day we were loaded onto a bus and taken on a field trip to a low-rent shopping mall. We walked by a shoe store, and I stopped in front of it, stunned. The styles had changed dramatically. The world had moved on without me. After only a few months I felt like an alien, out of touch and defeated, and withdrew further into myself.

My parents came to see me often and I was glad for that, although I was extremely depressed and saw nothing positive about life whatsoever. On the weekend of July 4, my dad picked me up so I could be at the Caribeth Drive house with them and their friends for their annual celebration. I was only able to last a few hours before succumbing to severe anxiety and needing to return to the hospital.

Three months passed, and I was still no better. I would probably be there to this day if the hospital hadn't announced that anyone there for longer than three months had to leave or be transferred to Camarillo State Hospital.

Camarillo State Hospital? The name alone evoked deep terror. The hospital was located about forty miles from Los Angeles and had the reputation of housing the insane. You rarely heard of anyone leaving the premises once they checked in. I knew I'd never survive there. I called my father the next morning and told him what the hospital had said. The next day he came to see me. Without my mother.

"Come home."

"No, Dad, I can't," I said, afraid to go home in my fragile state and fall victim to my mother's abuse.

"What do you have to lose? If it doesn't work out you can always go to Camarillo."

The wall I had built up in my mind was pretty thick, but somehow his words penetrated.

But I remembered having come home from the hospital on my July 4 visit. My parent's friends were having gay chatter around the pool, but I was experiencing intense anxiety and sat in a corner by myself. I had been unable to last more than a few hours before asking my father to take me back to the hospital. What made me think I'd be able to *stay* home?

On the Outside – 1967

The sweat poured off me. I was, quite simply, coming out of my skin.

"I need to scream," I said to my mother.

"So scream," she'd say.

And I would. Several times a day. And there was more. The ever-present anxiety made it impossible for me to be alone. So my mother could not leave me. My mother's health was stable for the moment, but it couldn't have been easy on her.

My anxiety might have tapered off if they hadn't been intolerant of me in ways that were detrimental to my well-being. I knew I needed psychiatric care and asked them for it. They laughed about psychiatrists while I sat there, feeling humiliated and adrift.

"They can't even cure their own problems," my mother said. "And they always blame the parents." Psychiatry at the time was still not embraced, but I was severely depressed and warranted serious help.

"They don't help anyone," my father insisted.

I didn't give up, pleading with them daily to take me to a psychiatrist, but was refused time and again.

One day my mother was in the kitchen, cutting up vegetables for dinner. I wandered in, looking for company.

Thoughts were colliding in my head, leading to mental paralysis. I was never sure if I was going to come out of it. Bridging the gap between these two worlds was often impossible and necessitated my waiting it out with the hope my brain would thaw. I couldn't speak at these times and my spirits plummeted.

"Are you feeling any better today, Lynn?" my mother asked.

I shook my head slowly.

She stood there a moment and looked at me. "If you're so sad all the time, you may as well kill yourself."

Rod – 2012

I was feeling creative again. It was almost Halloween.
I told Rod I would dress up for him. I asked him to tell me
his favorite color.

He said, "Deep blue like the ocean."

Then I typed:

STRIP CLUB

I'm taking you to a strip club. I make my way to
the stage and dance for you, and you alone. I am
wearing only a g-string and sexy bra in deep blue like
the ocean. There will be other men there, and they
will desire me also. But you will know the sexual
dancing is meant for you, and you alone, which gets
you aroused before I've even done anything.

I go to the pole and wrap my legs around it and
slide my pussy up and down to seductive music. You
become very hard, very fast. You want to touch

yourself, but I shake a finger at you not to do that. Then I step off the stage and approach you.

I offer you a lap dance and you accept, stuffing a few hundred-dollar bills in my g-string. I lower myself onto you. As I feel hard your cock beneath me I get very excited myself. I'm all the way down on your lap now and want badly to unzip your pants, but it's a nightclub and that's not allowed. So I swirl and circle my pussy and ass on your cock until you can't stand it. I whisper in your ear that I would like to take you in the private room.

When we're behind closed doors you unhook my bra and begin sucking on my erect nipples. You remove my g-string, and I reach down and unzip your pants to free your huge cock. As you begin thrusting that cock in and out of my tight, wet pussy, you fuck me like you've never fucked anyone and cum hard.

Rod's response:

Baby, you got me so incredibly hard. I would love to feel your pussy rubbing against my throbbing dick. I take your g-string off and then grab my cock and begin rubbing the head up and down your clit. The two of us are so aroused we can't wait any longer. I lay you back on the couch and throw your legs up over my shoulders as you guide my cock inside your pussy. I begin thrusting my cock deep and pounding your pussy hard. Neither of us have had a good fucking in quite some time. My cock

begins pulsating and throbbing, and explodes with
my hot cum shooting deep inside of your pussy as
your cum flows over my cock. Mmmm, I'm so
incredibly hot and horny.

This exchange of emails took the sex chats up a level.
We were now both being creative and inventing scenarios.
My mind was opening up, and I was eager to explore more
play with Rod.

He asked me again if we could talk on the phone; this
time I said yes. I was going to have phone sex for the first
time in my life. Was I supposed to say the same things I
said in the chats? Would I actually be able to voice those
things aloud?

From the moment Rod opened his mouth I knew I
didn't want phone sex with him. I didn't even want to talk
to him on the phone. He did not have the deep, sexy voice
I had imagined, and had an accent so thick I could barely
understand him. I couldn't identify the accent although he
said he lived in middle America. Are there accents there? I
had to keep asking him to repeat himself.

We got the preliminaries out of the way, such as: How
long have you been on this site? How do you like living
where you live? Have you ever been to California?) As
soon as the opportunity presented itself, I made my escape.
I was glad I called him as I had a blocked number. I did
not want to have to deal with the possibility of having to
talk with him again. Yet, he was a very sexually engaging
emailing partner so our chats online continued.

It's True, You Really Can't Go Home Again –
1967

I had in my possession a large quantity of pills. I could
have killed myself. Probably. Thoughts of the damage it
might do to my parents weren't a factor. My mother had
been the one to suggest it! I don't know why I didn't do it.
I wasn't one hundred percent sure I had enough meds to
complete the job, and I worried I might just become terribly
sick and suffer more. Slitting my wrists wasn't an option; I
wasn't into pain and what if I didn't succeed there? I
would have just made a mess and incurred more of my
mother's wrath. So I postponed it. I could always do it
later, I told myself. After all, there was no time limit on
suicide.

What I couldn't postpone was my response to what my
mother had said to me. It was more than feeling hurt. It
was grief on the deepest, most basic level. My mother had
told me she didn't believe my life was worth fighting for.

Eventually, my parents did decide on an action. They said they were taking me to get help. We piled in the car and drove over an hour to God knows where. The homes were getting far and few between and I was becoming concerned. What doctor would live out here?

I recall the house was very small. The woman who answered the door was elderly and frail. She invited us inside. She had me take a seat and then attempted to cure me by dangling vials of colored liquid in front of my face. My parents had taken me to a witch doctor! I couldn't wait to get out of there. I was frightened of never getting the help I needed.

∾

No matter how many times they turned me down, I continued to plead with my parents for a psychiatrist. They finally agreed to take me to see a psychologist, but I doubted he could help. I had been in the care of psychologists before and felt I needed in-depth analysis and possibly medication. I was to participate in group therapy. I felt I needed individual therapy. My problems were too deep for a group situation. Nonetheless, this was the only choice I had, the only therapy that was sanctioned by them, so I agreed.

Other parents visited group to see how they could be of help to their son or daughter and to hear them out. After about a month in therapy, I asked the doctor to invite my parents to a session. He called them and they agreed to come. For a few days I felt hopeful. There was that word again.

In the session, in front of the group, my parents ran off a list of everything they blamed me for, going all the way back to the time I was a young child and said "no" to everything; to not kissing my mother goodnight when I was fifteen, to when I was sixteen and wouldn't get the car washed for my father. These were obvious attempts at rebellion on my part to what I was going through at the time. After the session, the doctor took me aside and told me it was useless to have them back, that they were far too concerned with their own needs and expectations, and not enough about mine. Recently, someone who read this book asked if the doctor's validation registered with me. It did not. I was stuck in the muck and mire of psychological distress and couldn't internalize it. I felt estranged from myself.

I wanted to quit therapy. I wanted to quit life. My parents were never going to acknowledge that I needed love in a different way than they had been giving it, through gifts or taking me on trips. If I could only have accepted it, but how do you accept such a thing? I couldn't or wouldn't allow myself the realization that the fight for their love was hopeless. I just couldn't face it, and I don't think I ever did until their deaths.

Thinking back now, I sometimes fantasize that if there had been a master interpreter, an intermediary of supreme talents who could have dissected our behaviors like an autopsy of the mind, and then translated the results to each of us in great detail, maybe we could have comprehended what the other needed. But even that probably wouldn't have helped. What I needed was compassion, understanding, and support, but they couldn't give it. What they needed was a total acceptance of their criticism, mindless obedience, and adulation and it was destroying me. I felt desperately unloved.

~

For two months I had been frightened to drive anywhere by myself for fear of a panic attack. So I went nowhere. But finally I began to take baby steps, one street at a time, turning around at the faintest hint of anxiety. I dared not go beyond my comfort zone. But what was my comfort zone? It was different in every circumstance. There were mental roadblocks all over the city to prevent me from going anywhere.

I could not take freeways, only side streets, and just so far. If I were going into Los Angeles, I could not cross Fairfax Avenue. It was strictly prohibited in my mind, though I didn't know why. And I couldn't make left turns. That was absolutely forbidden, at least on major streets. I could manage them on residential streets if there was no one in front of me. Every destination had to be analyzed beforehand. But even so, sometimes I would be required to make an unexpected turn due to road construction or an accident. Every unplanned, unexpected turn could become, in my mind, a detour to hell.

Since I felt that great danger lay ahead if I veered from a prescribed route, I rarely did. Intentionally, anyway. It didn't matter that my own mind had created this network of roadblocks. The voices in my head directed me as to what was dangerous and what wasn't. And there was little that wasn't dangerous. I needed to be liberated from the voices, but I dared not negotiate with them. Defying the voices in any way could result in the ultimate punishment, a panic attack that would take me to *that* place, that far-off place from where I might never return. Where my mind would fragment into tiny little pieces. No, whatever the voices told me, I did or didn't do.

When I was able to complete a terrifying task, particularly where it related to driving, I thanked God and promised I'd never do it again, just like I used to do in Sun Valley. Strangely enough, I knew I wasn't crazy, but I had no control over my racing, threatening thoughts, and every time I got behind the wheel I feared that I might wind up stranded in an unfamiliar location, which could lead to becoming lost without hope of ever returning. Better not go. Better not try.

Even going to a movie was a journey filled with peril. Once inside the theater, I'd check the exits. *Can I get out quickly if the anxiety starts?* My heart was pounding in my chest. *Control the panic. Think of other things. Don't think at all! Take a deep breath. I can do it. Oh God, please...not now. Go or stay?* If I stayed, I might have a full-blown panic attack. If I left, I'd have given in to it. Finally I always left. Staying wasn't worth it. Nothing was. I made my escape. Whew! Relief! That time.

I may have been offered some comfort had I received a diagnosis of my problem, but none was given at the time. Today it would be diagnosed as agoraphobia.

~

Two months after I had moved home my father informed me that living with them wasn't working out, that two adult women couldn't live in the same house together. Of course I knew who was behind that decision. How could I live alone when I couldn't spend a single minute by myself? How would I get through the nights? Every time I went to sleep I thought I was going to die. In my head, sleep equaled death. Unanswerable questions about what might happen to me flooded my mind. Competing thoughts invaded my psyche; I can't make it, I have to make it.

Roommate – 1968

I advertised in the *Los Angeles Times* to find a
roommate; Lilly Grace, a nurse, answered it. We took an
apartment in a large complex in The Valley. I thought
when she got to know me she'd see through my attempt at
normalcy. But she never did.

I managed to secure a job as a receptionist for an
architectural firm. They too, seemed to accept me without
pause. A job and a roommate. Hope. Again.

Lilly was a great roommate, kind-hearted and friendly.
What started off very tentatively, on my part at least,
became a lifelong relationship. I consider myself very
lucky to have had her in my life.

During the year we lived together in The Valley, Lilly
met a man named Terrance Roberts, and they began dating.
When our lease was up, Lil found an apartment for the two
of us at a new complex in Marina del Rey. It was right on
the channel, had three pools, a deli, a dry cleaner, and a

very large recreation room. The grounds were lush. I was glad to be leaving The Valley, which I associated with so much of my unhappiness.

Lilly knew about my performing career, and for some reason she thought I wasn't through with it. I wondered how she knew that when I didn't know it myself. I'd been out of the hospital for two years by then, but couldn't imagine entertaining again. I'd lost all of my I've-got-it-in-spades attitude. Besides, there was no piano on which to practice and no money to buy one. So that was that.

And then one day I came home from my receptionist job and found a piano in the living room. Lilly had actually gone out and bought a used piano for me. No friend had ever shown such an extreme act of kindness toward me, and I've never forgotten it. I began to practice.

On weekends I'd visit my parents. Sometimes I'd bring a girlfriend, having met several likeable young women where we lived. Once I brought Julie, she was blond and buxom, with an outgoing personality. My father was warm and friendly to her when she was there, but later on he referred to her as a prostitute. I defended her vehemently, but the more I tried to talk sense into him, the more vociferous he became. I took an attack on my friend as an attack on me. My parents had long seemed obsessed with prostitution, though I would never know why. Anyone who was sexy, or who might enjoy sex, was likely to receive that label.

~

Terrance and Lilly continued to date during our first two years at Mariner's Village, while I sought work as an entertainer. Though jobs as a musician were always a challenge to get, gradually I got bookings again. I worked at every restaurant in Marina del Rey that had a piano. I sent out invitations by mail, and sometimes by phone, to my friends for both my openings and closings to bring in business so my employers would want to keep me longer. My friends provided new and repeat business, but for many establishments it wasn't enough to extend my contract. And since it is the nature of the entertainment business to change performers as often as every two weeks in some cases, I was constantly looking for work.

During our third year of living together, Terrance proposed to Lilly. After their honeymoon, both of them lived with me for a short time before finding their own apartment. After that, I had a succession of roommates, and jobs.

A young man who lived in the complex said, "Lynn, you are always either looking for a roommate, job, or boyfriend." And he was right.

I worked as a pianist/vocalist for a total of eight and a half years, a feat of sorts after having had only a total of five weeks of piano lessons and no vocal instruction. In the end, I was receiving more compliments on my voice than my piano playing. I was told it was sultry. What I had been most insecure about became my greatest asset.

An agent called me about an offer in Japan, but by that time I was tired of the pre-performance jitters, the constant searching for work, and the unstable income. I gave it up: the singing, playing, and composing. It had been a good run. Now I needed to confront how I was going to live my life from that point on.

NO RESERVATIONS – CIRCA 2012

A Short Story

Birthdays had a strange effect on me, especially his. By all accounts, he should have still been in my life. There was a fierce attraction and we loved each other.

I have never forgotten him nor have I stopped thinking about him, even though several years have passed.

But at that time I had reservations.

I chose my words carefully when I broke him up with him. I used the old standby, "It's not you, it's me. I'm just not ready to settle in (not *down*) with one person yet." Well, actually, it was true, sort of. I never mentioned age.

My husband had died five years before and it had been a long, protracted illness. I could see the terror in his eyes as he lay dying. I couldn't take a chance that I might have to face that again. I didn't want someone older; I wanted someone with youth on his side.

∼

Before I drift off to sleep at night I recall his hot breath between my legs, and how he smiled in anticipation of giving me pleasure. My nerve endings *there* tingle at the thought of him. He's still a part of me. I wonder if I am still a part of him. I'd like to find out, but how? I heard he's with someone else now, someone who apparently did want to settle in.

I yearn for his fingers to touch me again. I never had to tell him anything; he knew just what to do, what brought me to ecstasy. The right amount of pressure at the right place. And he was not afraid of being inappropriate. He just didn't have that gene! He'd take me in the backseat of his car sometimes when, as he said, he couldn't wait until we got home, that he had to have me that second. Oh, that feeling of being wanted that instant! The intensity of his desire for me was an intoxicant in itself. It created within me such a powerful response, I couldn't say no. I couldn't say anything. I'd just follow his lead.

I would pick up the phone to call him, then hang up before it rang.

Sure, there have been other men since. Younger men. Just like I wanted. But it wasn't the same. Not even close. He had the maturity to know what he wanted and the mettle to commit to it. He had the daring to take me places sexually I had never been before, and would never go to with another man. He showed me how exquisite true submission could be. I let him take me to the edge again and again.

He was a good teacher. He taught me how to use my mouth and my tongue in ways that would drive him wild, and yes, I loved having that power, to turn the tables, to watch him react as he climaxed finally, after I said it was okay, after I made him beg for it.

By all accounts he should have still been in my life. It would take pluck to contact him. He could say no, it's too late. But he needed to know. I'm a different woman now. I have no reservations.

Gabe, A Real Romance – 1972

I dated many men when I was single, but the only lengthy romance I had was with a man named Gabe.

We met at a singles bar in Beverly Hills. I was thirty and he was a few years younger. We saw each other on weekends and one night during the week. Gabe had a roommate, and occasionally we would double date. I could double date! I had a real boyfriend.

I was crazy about Gabe. He was a great lover and I enjoyed sex with him, although I still had the "prostitute" label in my head. Still, it was the most free I had felt sexually up to that point. Gabe wanted to please me, and he succeeded. I had orgasms through oral sex, and the fact that we were together for several nights in a week allowed for a sexual intimacy I had never had before. We got along great. But Gabe wasn't Jewish, and I was still under the influence of my parents about that. They wanted me to marry a Jewish man, and though we were never religious, they placed importance on this.

At age thirty, I still wanted my parent's approval; in fact, I needed it. I also wanted them to be proud of me. Marriage was the one area left that might elicit that, if I found someone I wanted to marry who wanted to marry me, and marry Jewish. But I was in love with Gabe. At that time, my friends and I looked at the fact that he was recently divorced and new on the dating market as a good thing.

I believed in true love, and I believed that if there was true love all obstacles, even religion, could be overcome. So I kept doing things I thought would make Gabe love me. I tried to be as cute, sexy, clever, and intelligent as possible. About six months had passed when one night Gabe called me and uttered the dreaded statement that I and every friend now fear if dating a recently divorced man: "I want to date other people."

Only in my case there was an add-on. "And you."

Actually, he just wanted to date one other woman, which I think was worse. *How long had he known her? How long had he been sleeping with her and deceiving me?*

I was, purely and simply, brokenhearted. He wanted to alternate weekends, one weekend me, the other her. I said I couldn't do it. Only due to the help and encouragement of my friends, and their listening to me go on about Gabe was I able to maintain my distance from him. And Gabe didn't help matters, he kept calling me, still wanting to see me.

A few times I relented. So strong were my feelings it was very difficult to resist him. I remembered how good the sex was and sometimes I succumbed, but not always because I had the strength of my friends behind me. If I hadn't, I wouldn't have lasted a day.

Still, life had to go on. I joined a gym in Century City and started my own business, a legal secretarial service. I rented a space in a suite occupied solely by attorneys. They kept me busy with work. I did the work quickly and accurately, and they appreciated that. I liked being my own boss. I was a hard worker and very ambitious.

One night after working out at the gym, I was sitting in the lobby of the club to rest before heading home to the Marina. Much to my surprise, Gabe's roommate walked in. I hadn't known he belonged; I had never seen him there. He sat down and we talked for a few minutes. It had been about eight months since I'd seen Gabe, and I was determined I would not ask about him. But I didn't have to.

"Did you know Gabe is engaged?" he asked casually.

I felt hot, sweaty, and weak. If I hadn't been sitting down, I'm sure I would have fainted. How could he be marrying someone else? Didn't we have the best relationship possible? What about our great sex life? It was a tremendous shock to me and one I never forgot, although the impact waned with time. But the question tormented me for a long time: Why didn't he marry me?

Jerry – 1980

My search to find a new relationship continued. It had been six years since I learned Gabe was getting married. I didn't think about him anymore except in the context of the last time I had a boyfriend.

Eventually I had to give up my typing service, business having dried up, and I returned to an earlier occupation: legal secretary. Fortunately I found work in the Marina, five minutes from where I lived. I finally had my very own apartment. No more roommates! No matter how compatible a roommate might have been, Lilly being the best hands down, you never have the same freedom as when you're alone.

One Friday night, an old roommate invited me to meet her and her boyfriend for drinks at the private Marina City Club. I was tired after a long workweek and really didn't want to go, but as usual, I went in spite of how I felt on the off chance that I would meet someone.

The lounge was overflowing with people; standing room only at the bar, and all the booths were filled. I scouted the room for my ex-roommate. We caught each other's eye and I headed in her direction, but on the way I met a man with a fabulous smile, and we hit it off. His name was Jerry Rosenberg. I told him I had to say hi to my friend, but that I'd be back.

My girlfriend and her boyfriend were doing just fine, so I returned to the bar, where Jerry and I resumed our lively conversation. Two hours passed quickly, but I was getting tired and prepared to leave. Jerry said he was ready to call it a night also, so we walked to the elevator together and continued outside to our cars. Then he invited himself over to my apartment so he wouldn't have to drive back to his, which was forty-five minutes away. I had heard a lot of reasons why a man wanted to stay overnight with me, but none as lame as this one. I said goodnight to him at my car and told my parents that weekend that I had met one of the biggest jerks of my dating life.

On Saturday night the following week, I was to pick up a girlfriend from the airport. I stopped at a restaurant called Donkins to kill time before her flight arrived. Many of my friends had met their husbands there. For the last decade it had been a hub for singles. I even sang and played there at one point. But now it was on its last legs, not only as a singles bar, but as a restaurant too.

As I entered, I spotted two nice-looking men at one of the communal round tables near the bar. They were the only people in the room, so I sat down at their table and said hi. The dark-haired one offered to buy me a drink. Somewhere in between the ordering of the drink and its arrival, I realized that I had met this man the week before at the Marina City Club. It was Jerry Rosenberg. I was surprised to see him again. I had a more favorable impression of him this time. He was dressed better than he had been before and wasn't as aggressive. They invited me to join them for dinner but I had already eaten. So they insisted I come along, if only for a drink.

I enjoyed talking with Jerry. He had a handsome face and a beautiful, broad smile. He asked me if I'd like to get together later. Here it was again, the push to get in my pants. I said I was sorry, but no, it would be too late. He asked me for my phone number, and I gave it to him. I figured he'd never call, having been turned down twice.

Ever since my days of performing, my friends knew not to phone me before noon, and even though I wasn't singing and playing anymore, the rule still applied on weekends. So when I was awakened at 9:30 the next morning by the telephone ringing, the person on the other end of the line was in serious jeopardy to be sure. Groggily, I answered the phone. It was Jerry Rosenberg inviting me for breakfast. I broke my own rule. I didn't get mad. I got dressed.

I had a great time at breakfast. Jerry was funny, and I laughed a lot. I was interested in him on several levels. He was part of a large family which I liked and had missed out on as an only child. He was a builder and developer, an entrepreneur, and that's how I thought of myself, regardless of my return to secretarial work. He was physically appealing to me. So with all this, naturally I didn't think I would ever hear from him again. But I did, and we began dating.

I had entered analysis with a psychiatrist, who was seeing me for a low fee, just three weeks before meeting Jerry. I saw this doctor four times a week for depression and anxiety. Jerry and I began dating each other regularly and I attributed our connecting to the help I was receiving from my psychiatrist. I don't think I would have been able to construct, let alone maintain, a relationship without his help. I had no trust in men, which I only realized through my sessions with this doctor, and I feared them. And I certainly didn't trust myself, which my doctor was also able to help me with.

A month after we met, Jerry invited me to go away with him for the weekend to Palm Springs. Though I was thirty-six, this was the first time I had ever gone away with a man. I had stopped taking birth control pills to give my body a rest and resumed taking them the day before we went away. It was the end of May and it was very hot in the desert. Jerry loved to play tennis, and when he was finished, he'd join me in the pool. I treasured this time with him.

Soon Jerry wanted me to meet his daughter, Darlene. He had a son, but he didn't live locally. Though Jerry's ex-wife had come to terms with their divorce and even had a boyfriend, I was very nervous about meeting Darlene because daughters are known to be protective of their fathers. I was concerned she might be jealous of me and I didn't want to elicit negative feelings. But Jerry told me not to worry about Darlene at all, that she would be completely welcoming of me, and he was right. Darlene was warm and friendly, and very open toward her father having a woman in his life.

Not long after meeting Darlene, Jerry wanted me to meet one of his sisters, and from what he told me, it was rare for him to take a woman to meet a member of his family. I was very excited. Jerry had just bought me roller skates, and we skated over to the beach. My father was unimpressed, professing his preference that Jerry buy me a diamond. His sister had a second home, a condo, facing the ocean in Marina del Rey. She and her husband were warm and friendly to me, and I felt encouraged that Jerry would bring me to meet them.

One of Jerry's nieces was getting married in what was to be one of the exciting Las Vegas social events of the year. Their parents were all important members of the Las Vegas community. I thought it would be fun to go to the wedding together. He called his relatives on my behalf, but no amount of charm or persuasion on his part would change their minds. Unless I was married to a member of the family I could not go. I had never heard of anything like this, but it was their family and their choice, whatever the reason. Jerry received an invitation for one.

My Period Was Late – 1980

I struggled to zip up my pants. My battle not to regain the same ten pounds over and over again was never far from my mind, but because I didn't think I was eating more than normal, I couldn't make sense of it. The birth control pills had provided me protection for years; surely they wouldn't fail me now. I saw my gynecologist, and while he didn't test me, he didn't think I was pregnant either. So a strict diet was in order.

When I didn't have a period for almost four months, I returned to my gynecologist, fearing there was something wrong with me. This time he informed me that I was pregnant and sixteen weeks pregnant at that. I was stunned to learn this news, let alone that I was that far along. I considered myself an intelligent woman. How could this happen? If someone else had told me they didn't suspect they were pregnant after four months without a period, I would have said they were either insane or incredibly stupid. And I was on birth control pills, for God's sake!

Jerry was not only uninterested in getting married, he was impassioned against having more children. And I had serious reservations about being a mother after being told by my parents that if they had to do it all over again they would not have had children. Thanks for sharing, Mom and Dad. If raising a child was that awful, why would I want to do it? Worse, what if I turned into dear old Mom, who couldn't love her own child?

I spoke to Jerry at length about it and he was clear. No more children.

But this child was growing inside me. I experienced a flood of mixed emotions, suddenly yearning to bond with this child, to nurture and love it. But I was single, and had an emotional and financial history to consider. I anguished over the possibility of having an abortion.

I took myself out to the local pizzeria for dinner. There I sat, quietly, just my unborn baby and me. I observed people coming and going but the only life that really mattered was the one growing inside me. For the moment, it was enough.

There must be some way I could have this child, I told myself. But when I looked at the reality of the whole picture, I didn't feel capable of raising a child without a partner.

I had the desire to tell my parents about the pregnancy but I couldn't bring myself to do so, fearing they would provoke more guilt than I was already experiencing. I chose the next best person, a lifelong family friend, Angie.

I needed to talk to someone. A few days later, my mother called as Angie had called her. My mother was not unkind, but chances are she would have been if Angie had not been a benevolent intermediary.

Because I was so far along, I had to have the abortion in a hospital. Jerry and Darlene came to visit me, as did my mother and father. I thought about how my parents might feel, losing the only grandchild they may ever have. But I also had made up my mind that any child of mine would not be exposed to the same distorted thinking and behaviors that I experienced. In the end though, regarding this child, my parents would have to deal with it in the same way that I had to: a tragic loss, plain and simple.

My mother offered to spend the night with me in the hospital. Being that all of my life she had been so cold to me, I was touched by her offer and I accepted it. This was by far the kindest thing emotionally she'd ever done for me. She didn't even have her insulin with her. She could have fallen into a diabetic coma, but she never mentioned it.

A cynic might say, "Well, she was in a hospital, if she needed insulin her doctor could order it," but I took it for what I believed it was, the one true and loving kindness my mother ever showed me.

That weekend I recuperated at my parent's home.

"Wouldn't it be funny if you and Jerry wound up getting married?" my mother asked.

"Yes, it would," I answered, having a glimmer of hope that that might happen, though I had no idea why.

Jerry phoned to find out how I was feeling. I believed he genuinely cared about me. But early the following week, something about how he described what he'd done over the weekend told me that he had been with another woman, while I was recovering from my abortion. This hurt me deeply.

When I was back in my own place, and recovered, I told Jerry I was going to start seeing other people.

"I thought you were already," he said.

Well, I hadn't been and I wasn't about to start. I simply wasn't interested. But as far as he knew, I was.

Months passed and despite Jerry thinking that I was going out with others, every time we were together our affection for each other grew deeper. It wasn't long before Jerry moved in with me. I loved having him there. I still couldn't go to a Rosenberg wedding, but I was getting closer!

Jerry was everything I wanted. He was funny, caring, loving, handsome, came from a good family, and had ambition. It would have been wonderful if we had been a match in bed, too, but it was not to be.

And for my part, I couldn't make love the way I had with Gabe. I think there were many reasons why Jerry and I didn't click sexually, and my inhibition was one of them. I was trained that I'd be thought of as a prostitute if I was too enthusiastic or creative when it came to sex, let alone if I enjoyed it. I didn't want Jerry to think of me that way, or to think of myself that way. Above all, I needed to be "good," especially with a man who really cared about me.

We lived together for nine months, and suddenly one day it occurred to me that Jerry would probably continue to live in my apartment without ever asking me to marry him if I let him. And that's when I decided to pull the plug. I told him either I would need a proposal or he'd have to move out. It was a big gamble. He hadn't wanted a child and he'd certainly stuck to his guns about that, so there was every possibility he would hold strong with his conviction not to marry and move out. I remembered the aching loneliness I had felt when Gabe and I broke up. This would be ten times worse. Despite the lack of a great sexual connection, Jerry and I loved each other.

Love in Bel Air – 1981

At thirty-eight, after waiting all those years and seeing
every girlfriend I ever had get married, it was my turn.
Jerry asked me to marry him.

I could make this commitment to Jerry because, unlike
my parents, he did not need to place restraints on me. He
didn't greet me with, "Where have you been?" or "Why are
you late?" but rather, "Hi, honey!" or "Hi, sweetheart!" and
"Did you have a good day?" never grilling me about
insignificant details. I could breathe with him.

I was always very careful what I told my mother,
conveying only what I thought she wouldn't find fault with,
but sometimes she would still surprise me. I had
mentioned that one of Jerry's brothers and his wife
belonged to El Caballero Country Club, a golf club where
several of my mother's friends belonged.

A few days later, while discussing my upcoming
wedding, my mother told me that her friend, who knew

Jerry's brother, had never mentioned that there was another brother. "He must be the black sheep of the family," my mother said.

This wounded me deeply, one of the endless cuts into the fabric of my soul, but I could say nothing. If I argued with my mother, she would tell me I was upsetting her and that she could go into a diabetic coma or worse. Then she would report it to my father, who would have it out with me as well.

A few months before the wedding, in a burst of enthusiasm, I told my mother I had chosen a beautiful gown for my special day. She asked if she could see it, "Not to say yes or no," just to see it. Nothing would have pleased me more than to show it to her, were she a loving presence in my life. I mumbled a consent, but I didn't follow through. This was the one time in my life that I couldn't allow myself to acquiesce. That dress was perfect in my eyes, and I couldn't take the chance that a slight gesture, or question, or disapproving look from her would ruin it for me. I did not make the decision lightly and have often thought about it since. This is the only regret I have with regard to my mother. And yet it can't really be called a regret, because if given the opportunity to do it over again, I would choose to do the same thing. It was a matter of self-preservation.

$\sim$

I had the wedding of my dreams. I chose the Bel Air Hotel, a magnificent site in Bel Air, California. Swans floated in streams, low-slung branches of California sycamore trees caressed wooden pathways, and an elegant calm settled in.

A light drizzle had been predicted. I worried that it might be cold, but I needn't have been concerned. People pay good money to live there, millions, in fact. For that, they get prime Bel Air weather—not overcast like the ocean, nor arid like The Valley. Wedding-day-perfect weather every day.

I had the works: full-length bridal gown with shoulder-length veil, Jerry's daughter Darlene was my maid of honor, and the flower girl Sarah was Lilly and Terrance's daughter. My mother had been too ill to participate in the planning of the wedding, so I did everything myself and I loved every minute of it, including: the wedding invitations (the year was accidently left off); designing the chuppah, the structure under which we would stand to take our vows (a different shape than what I had created); choosing the cake flavor and height (four tiers, yellow flowers on white icing prepared as ordered); and violinists who performed beautifully when the band took a break.

What wasn't perfect was still perfect.

My parents paid for the wedding except for a small amount that Jerry contributed.

Jerry and I had prepared a slide show. This was before videos became popular for weddings and bar mitzvahs, so it was truly a novelty. Together we picked out photographs from our year-and-a-half relationship and turned them into slides. I wrote a six-page script, and we acted out our parts and prerecorded it. We had a friend of Jerry's run the slide show right before I walked down the aisle. Our friends and relatives laughed and shed a few tears. It was both touching and funny, and a big hit. It brought everyone together. As Dad walked me down the aisle, which wasn't easy for him since arthritis had taken its toll, I noticed Angie's face light up. I could tell she was thrilled for me. She reflected the love I had always hoped to see in my mother's face.

The moment that Jerry and I were called to the floor for our first dance as husband and wife was exhilarating. I was finally married! A side benefit of marrying Jerry: I could now go to all the Rosenbergs' events. I was a Rosenberg! Brown no more. While I should have been able to do this for myself but was never able to, I could now allow myself the luxury of feeling good about myself. Somebody loved me.

The next morning we flew to Manzanillo, Mexico for a weeklong honeymoon, which was beautiful and romantic. And I had the best sex of our relationship that first afternoon of our trip. Jerry was really into satisfying me, and I let myself go. If only both had lasted. I told him how much I enjoyed having sex with him, and he responded with what I thought was a strange comment: "Just don't get used to it."

Mother – The Final Chapter – 1982

Until the day my mother died, I had hoped that
somehow she would come around. I hoped she would
apologize for threatening to abandon me, that she would
ask forgiveness for all the times she undermined me, and
for a lifetime of emotional abuse. But she never did. On
her deathbed she reminisced about my Sweet Sixteen
birthday party at the Tail o' the Cock. Though it was one
of the happier events of my youth and a poignant memory,
it had long since been overshadowed by her hostile
treatment.

She made no apologies. She did not ask for
forgiveness. And so fearful was I of my mother's rebuke,
that even though I was thirty-eight years old when my
mother was dying, I never had the courage to ask her,
"Why didn't you ever tell Dad the truth about your
threatening to send me away?" or "Why did you never
apologize?"

At the time it happened, of course, I didn't know it was only a threat. I thought she was really going to send me away and that it was my hysteria that saved me. From then on, when things got really bad, I relied on the fact that maybe if I screamed loudly enough and cried hard enough, I had a chance of getting my way, and surviving. She did tell me she wished me a happy life with Jerry, which I appreciated.

I had been anticipating the death of my mother and father nearly my entire life. "Nobody will ever love you like we do," they would say. I tried to ward off that statement and discard it from my mind. I hadn't wanted to believe it. But it stuck. And then I'd ask myself, *If they are the only ones who will ever love me, how can I possibly function on my own when they are gone?*

Moments before my mother died I said to her, "I don't know how Dad's going to get along without you."

"You'll just have to help him," she answered. But I knew my father wouldn't accept my help. He was too resentful of me, convinced I'd made my mother's life a living hell, not the other way around.

After years of on-and-off hospitalizations, shots every day into her deformed thighs, and decades of trying to balance insulin versus sugar, with her eyesight worsening and suffering on dialysis, my mother wanted out. But my father wouldn't listen to her pleas. He couldn't let her go and kept her alive against her wishes, not agreeing to her desire to stop dialysis and come home to die. At her last hospitalization, she begged me to bring her pills so she could kill herself.

"I can't do that," I said, aghast that she would ask that of me. Too many times my words were twisted, too many times I felt guilt over aggravating her, and too many times my father regurgitated the fact that during a certain period of my teenage years I did not kiss her goodnight.

"That hurt your mother deeply." My father never forgave me for that.

There was no way I was going to help her kill herself. Maybe it's because I didn't love her enough. Maybe it's because I didn't want more guilt on my head added to all the other guilt I felt toward her. Whatever the reason, I wasn't going to do it. I didn't even give any thought to the fact that I'd probably wind up in prison, nor apparently had she.

Finally, my father agreed to let her come home one final time. At age fifty-nine, ten months after Jerry and I were married, my mother died. For one brief moment, when I realized I would never again have the chance to prove myself worthy of her love, I felt heartbroken, but after that moment passed I felt nothing. If I had to attribute any emotion to her loss, it would be relief, knowing I would never be demeaned by her again. But I don't think I even felt that.

Because I had Jerry in my life, and the benefit of what I saw as his real, true love, I did not, in the end, fear for my emotional survival as I once had.

My father, on the other hand, was bereft. I could hear him wail from the other end of the house. He was also angry, which he expressed by being belligerent to everyone, even his close friends who came over to the house to grieve with him. He was angry that he'd lost her, angry that he was now alone, angry at me for what he perceived as my not loving her, and angry that my mother had suffered physically the way she did. There was no way to know for sure, but I suspected he could not allow himself to think about the fact that he himself prolonged her suffering by extending her life against her wishes because he couldn't bear to be without her. If he had faced that, he might have felt some anger toward himself.

A few months later, although he was still grief-stricken, friends were able to talk him into going out for dinner. There was no question whether my father would marry again. He stated vehemently that if something happened to my mother he would never remarry. He might as well have had it tattooed on his arm, that's how resolved he was.

Two months after that, he told me his friend Rebecca had set him up on a date with a woman she had met at the beauty salon. My father took the woman out a few times, and then he called me and said he would like it if I came to meet her.

Despite the heart-wrenching relationship I had endured with my mother, I found myself furious that after the protestations over all the years that my father would never be with another woman, in spite of sacrificing me repeatedly on the altar of my mother's shrine, here he was with another woman he wanted me to meet! I wondered what my mother would have thought, given my father's repeated promises that there would never be another woman in his life, that he had found one in less than six months.

Jerry and I met my dad and Lee at a restaurant in West Hollywood that was showcasing gay performers who sang songs from *La Cage aux Folles* and other musicals. I know how this is going to sound, but from the moment I saw Lee I didn't like her. I resented her taking my mother's place so quickly. I tried to put on my party face, but the rage was probably visible right below the surface.

Four weeks later, Lee moved into my mother's home. Yes, I know, it was my dad's home also.

Lee was very beautiful. She had been a stand-in for Elizabeth Taylor, and she was constantly getting compliments over the similarity. Gradually, I came to like Lee, even love her. But that came later.

$\sim$

My father's rage did not dissipate. And when he was angry he could be terrifying, to me at least. I watched every word I said as usual, but even that was not enough.

One evening, a few months after my mother died, my father wanted to meet Jerry and me for dinner so he could give me Mother's jewelry. We suggested the Marina City Club, where Jerry and I had met and still frequented. At that time the club had a coffee shop, and that's where Dad wanted to eat.

After we finished dinner, Dad took out the jewelry. "You don't deserve it," my father said to me. His voice was loud enough for others in the restaurant to hear.

"Dad, please—"

"You never cared about your mother," he said, his voice still raised.

"That's not true," I answered.

"The only reason I'm giving it to you is that your mother wanted you to have it. I don't know why, the way you treated her."

People in the restaurant were looking our way. I was embarrassed and humiliated. I couldn't make eye contact with him.

"Phil, keep your voice down," Jerry said.

"You don't know anything about this, Jerry," my father snapped.

My head was spinning. I was suddenly a child again, unwilling to defend myself for fear of even worse abuse.

"You never gave your mother or me a moment's happiness."

I had heard this before, but it was no less upsetting each subsequent time. There are many standout moments in my life that vie for top place on the list of the times and ways I was most humiliated by my parents, and this I believe, is the winner.

Ultimately, he gave me the jewelry, but I felt I had paid a price for it. Later, when I decided to sell a piece of it

and buy myself a gold-and-diamond watch I truly loved
and felt would provide a better memory of my mother than
if I had kept, but not enjoyed her jewelry, Dad was furious
at me. He also gave me Mother's mink coat. It was too
small for me so I had it reworked into a jacket. I wore it
one evening when he and Lee, and Jerry and I went, out to
dinner. My father was so enraged at me for altering the
coat that I never wore it again in his presence.

A few years before my father died he confessed he
always felt guilty toward my mother for his treatment of
her. I thought this was quite an admission. But I warned
myself to tread lightly lest I be pounced upon.

"Why?" I asked. "Because you were so devoted to
your mother while she was alive and neglected Mother's
feelings?"

He acknowledged this was true. I experienced a
moment of wishful thinking. I thought his observance of
this and openly expressing it might lead him to realize his
part of the family dynamics that caused me, and my mother
for that matter, damage. But it only lasted a second; then
he was back to his old domineering, distrustful self that left
not the slightest hint of compassion or understanding
toward me.

ONE TIME ONLY—CIRCA 2012

A Gay Short Story

I wasn't looking to meet anyone. I had just
broken up with a guy half my age. I should have
known better, but I was addicted to his dick. Long
and very thick, every time I wanted to break it off
with him he'd whip it out – always hard and ready to
go. I needed that cock in my mouth and in my ass.
So I let the relationship go on for a year. Matt was
also good with repairs. Anything that needed fixing,
he dove right in and took care of it. I was busy
playing psychologist while he kept my aging house
and my aging body from falling apart.

I was only forty-nine, not so old, but I did not
keep my body up the way I should have. Sure I went
to the gym, but I could have been more buff than I
was. I had the drive to be a good shrink but less so a

real stud. I worked out but I didn't push myself. I
didn't eat that well, either. Matt, on the other hand,
was a vegetarian, exercised every day, and had a
model-perfect body. Well, he had the time and, let's
face it, the discipline. He was a wannabe actor.
Every now and then he'd get work, a small role,
maybe some extra jobs, but for the most part I
supported him. Which was fine with me. As long as
he was in my life I wanted him to be happy. Wanted
to keep that cock from wandering. In spite of my
efforts, I knew Matt had other men. He never told
me but I knew. And I knew we wouldn't last. It
wasn't just the age difference. I was cerebral and
fairly satisfied with my life. Matt was ever
searching, restless, undefined. I knew once he met
some wild man, someone on the edge, he would leave
me. But I was determined to enjoy him as long as it
lasted.

And then one day it happened. He told me he
met someone else, that he was sorry and appreciative
of all I'd done for him, but this other man was a news
reporter who had assignments in distant places and
had plans to take Matt with him. I should have been
prepared. I took it hard. And I was surprised to find
myself both angry and lonely. Maybe it wasn't just
his cock. Maybe I really cared for him, certainly
more than I thought.

I found my concentration lagging at work. I
feared my patients would pick up on it. Thoughts of

Matt kept invading my mind. I was concerned my interest in my charges might be waning and even wondered if I was fit to be a psychologist. Not only did I have doubts about myself as a therapist, but I was having questions about my desirability.

One night I came home to face another night of loneliness (I wasn't into bars) and found my sink had overflowed. Water everywhere. My newly replaced dining and living room carpets were soaking wet. I nearly slipped on the kitchen tile. The place was a mess.

With Matt gone, I was left to figure out this crisis on my own. Find someone in the phone book? Call a friend to get a reference? I remembered one of my neighbors recently had a toilet that overflowed. I pulled out my cell and called her.

"This guy's great," she said. "If anyone can fix it, he can."

I took the number down and dialed. He arrived twenty minutes later. I don't know how he did it. I lived on the west side of Los Angeles. I knew he lived in Burbank. The drive usually takes an hour when traffic is moving. However he managed it, I needed rescuing and I was glad to see him arrive so quickly. He had a closely-cropped beard, and a very neat and clean appearance. Impressive for someone in his line of work.

"Wow, this *is* a mess," he said. "Hi, I'm Greg."

"Hi, I'm Dave. Think you can fix it?" I asked.

"Give me a minute to see what the problem is,
but I'm sure I can. I've fixed worse than this."

"Worse than this?" I asked.

"The whole house was flooded. I needed to call
two other guys."

He went to his car for some equipment. Within
minutes the floor and carpet were dry.

"I have to replace a broken pipe. Actually, this
is pretty bad. I will need to call those two other guys
I mentioned."

"Call whomever you need," I said, relieved he
knew what the problem was and that he and his
buddies could repair it.

The two other men showed up quickly, also.
Watching a team of muscular guys using pure,
visceral strength to improve my surroundings
suddenly made me think of sex. These guys were
well-built, not toned from working out at the gym
like Matt, but firm bodies from manual labor. I was
aroused and had fantasies of wanting them all to take
turns sucking my cock and fucking my ass. I
suddenly forgot about Matt and about whether I was
desirable or not. They were friendly and joked with
me while they worked. One winked at me. His name
was Reggie. Reggie was the only man of color. He
was in his late twenties. The other two were about
my age. Between his swagger and smile, Reggie had
the look of a guy who pretty much got whatever he
went after.

"Did you have plans to have company over tonight?" Reggie asked.

The question took me by surprise.

"No ... I didn't. Why?"

"Because this may set your plans back by a few hours."

"Take as long as you need. I'm in no hurry," I answered.

In fact I was glad to have them around. Before now, I'd never been attracted to three men at once. Sure, in fantasy, but not in reality. Reggie had a full, sensual mouth. I kept picturing it wrapped around my cock, sucking me off. He was tall, like me. I liked tall men. They were usually confident, especially sexually. Maybe it was just my experience, but it always worked for me.

The other man spoke up. "Hey, I'm Austin."

Austin was gorgeous. High cheekbones, dark eyes, black hair way too long, falling into his eyes. I had the urge to sweep that hair off his face and kiss him with full tongue.

I wondered if Reggie, Austin, and Greg were thinking what I was thinking? Foursome. Just the thought made my cock rock-hard and it wasn't long before my boxers felt wet. Precum is almost always instant with me. I didn't want to appear too eager so I spoke silently to my cock, trying to persuade it to calm down. It wasn't working. As long as I was sitting I was okay. But if I stood up I'd give myself away immediately.

It was three hours before they completed the job. It was late. I wondered how to approach them. They were packing up their equipment and I had to think fast.

"Well, that's it. I think you'll be okay from here on out," said Greg, as he handed me the bill. I blinked but didn't say a word. They were worth it, and what was my choice, anyway?

I went to my desk, pulled out my checkbook, and put pen to paper. As I ripped the check out, I said, trying to sound smooth, "The least I can do for all the work you've done is buy you guys a beer."

"What do you think?" Greg asked the others.

"Sure why not?" they both echoed.

Reggie and Austin sat on the sofa, each on one side of me. Greg sank into a nearby chair.

Nearly finished with our second beer, I put on some music, questioning myself why I waited so long to do it. "I've got some quality weed," I said.

"Great," Austin said. A half-hour later, Austin would express himself by tapping my leg casually. "What do you like, Dave?"

"I'm not sure what you mean."

"C'mon, you like to dance first or to be touched?"

This was what I was waiting for. The opening I didn't have the courage to make. I responded by doing what I had wanted to do all night…shove that hair back off his face and kiss him open-mouthed. He moaned. Reggie and Greg did, too. It was going to happen. In moments, I was surrounded. Legs and arms leaning into me. I was so excited I was afraid I'd cum too soon.

"I've got a nice big bed," I managed.

"Let's go for it," Greg said.

We were in various states of undress when Reggie grabbed my cock and started sucking. No one's ever sucked me like that before, not even Matt, the best lover I had ever had. Something about Reggie's intent to satisfy. He focused on the tip to start, then took me in deep. I could only hope to keep control so I would fully be able to enjoy the experience of being in the arms, mouth, and ass of the three men. I just made up my mind: nothing was going to keep me from reveling in this. But my anticipation was building into a sense of sheer excitement I hadn't felt in...maybe ever. Being sucked and fucked by three men, one after the other, sometimes all at once, was almost too much for my meek soul to comprehend.

Austin, though the shortest man, had the biggest cock. And I thought tall men were Gods! Licking and sucking his pulsing dick created a desire in me to satisfy all of them. I tried to take both Austin's and Greg's cocks in my mouth but when that didn't work, I alternated my attention between the two as Reggie continued sucking me with abandon, using tongue now and then to bring me to a frenzied state of arousal.

Withdrawing for just a second, Reggie said, "I want you to come in my mouth."

"After I fuck you," I whispered in a low, soft voice I never heard from myself before.

Reggie's eyes pierced mine. "Okay, baby, whatever you want."

Before the night was out, I fucked and sucked each of them and I came in Reggie's mouth, just like he wanted. I should say I exploded in his mouth. I've never been so fired up in any sexual encounter. This was one to write home about – if one could write home about such a thing.

When it was all over, we said our thank-yous and shook hands. I knew we'd never see each other again, but it was a hell of a one-time only. One I would never forget.

Hello Mrs. Rosenberg - 1981

The first several years of my marriage to Jerry were all
I could have hoped for. I loved being married. Before we
were married I decided to try my hand at screenwriting and
took some classes. I had seen so many awful movies that I
thought I could do better. So I'd write during the day and
look forward to having Jerry come home to me every night
for dinner. I was playing house for real. Jerry was a real
estate developer and working on a potentially big project in
Denver, and we were very excited about it.

But the sex continued to be unsatisfying. Even at age
forty-two, I felt that my wanton desires were something to
be suppressed. Never during our marriage would I stroke
myself to climax after our unfulfilling love-making. Rarely
did I feel I could discuss my physical needs with him. I
had the man of my dreams in my loving arms, yet my self-
confidence was still shackled; I could not speak with Jerry
honestly about our sex life and neither could he. And I

never knew what he meant by that odd statement he made on our honeymoon. He may have been kidding, but I had difficulty shaking it off. What I lost by my reticence I could not regain.

~

My days were spent writing screenplays, and honing my craft to the best of my ability. I went to a script consultant who helped me immensely. She was nurturing, warm, encouraging, and generous, and we became close friends.

Life was smoothing out a little. Dad wasn't as angry. Lee was a very ingratiating woman and charmed her way into everyone's heart. Not only was she beautiful, but she had a fun, playful personality, and a way of making you feel important. But as time went on, events in her personal story didn't make sense, and happenings in her daily life weren't cohesive. I wasn't sure what to believe. She had told us that her husband and four-year-old son had died in a car crash. That wasn't the problem. That she only had a single photograph of them at a distance, was. She explained it away by saying that all her photographs had been in storage and the storage bin had burned to the ground.

I asked if her in-laws had any photographs. She said they had both died in a fire.

In her daily life, there were inconsistencies. But they were small and gradual. Nothing was pronounced enough to make you want to scream, "Liar!" But my head would shake, and often.

~

Real estate plunged into a downward cycle. Money came in sporadically. Even if the project in Denver became a reality, it could be years before we'd see any money. Still, we managed to hire an inexpensive interior designer and make some improvements to our apartment. Here's where going into business with my parents could have helped, if I could have done it without losing my mind. We lived in a two-bedroom apartment that directly overlooked one of the keys populated by boats of all shapes and sizes in Marina del Rey. We entertained frequently, sipping drinks on our patio, barbequing turkey, and enjoying our lives. It was all very simple, but wonderful.

We were also able to do some traveling. A few months after our honeymoon in Mexico, we visited England for a week, then went to Greece for a cruise. For the first time in my life sex was available to me any time I wanted it. If only I had wanted it. My inhibitions ran rampant. I couldn't take a chance of associating myself with anything that might suggest prostitution, or as my parents might have defined it - the joy of sex, in my marriage.

Jerry would try in his way. Sometimes he wanted to watch porn, but I refused. At the time my view was, why wasn't I enough? And I was judgmental. Who watched porn, anyway? Sick people. People who couldn't enjoy sex for what it was, an expression of love between two people. Today of course, I see it as a way to add an extra layer of eroticism to a relationship.

Admittedly, I was closed-minded, and not just to porn. One day I was filling the bath with water, and Jerry asked if he could join me. I made some poor excuse that I was tired and just needed to be by myself, but really, I didn't want to open myself up sexually to him. And yet despite what we lacked sexually together, I had never known what it was to be loved before Jerry. He genuinely cared about me, and starved as I was for love, that was more meaningful than anything, including sex. From Jerry's point of view, all I know is that he never expressed unhappiness with me or resentment of any kind.

Bora Bora – 1984

I had been fearful of a panic attack before we left
home. I pictured myself stuck on a tiny island with no way
out. The thing that intrigued me was the thing that
frightened me: its remoteness. But I wanted to go, so I
fought it, hoping blindly that it wouldn't happen to me. I
had a prescription from my therapist to take with me, but I
knew the medication would just numb me and would take a
long time to squelch the panic.

The small plane landed us on a tiny strip of land called
a *motu*. After stretching our legs and trying to cope with
the extreme heat, we boarded a motorboat and headed for
Bora Bora. We then climbed aboard a bus that took us to
the Bora Bora Hotel, a lodge-inspired resort overlooking a
breathtaking expanse of turquoise-colored water. The hotel
was completely open-air. No windows or doors, just a
spectacular vista with a 180-degree view of the sea.

We had not yet been able to secure a hut over the

water, so the first night we settled into a garden room. We had dinner at the hotel and then, saturated by the heat, returned to our abode. We had been back only a few moments when I was overcome with a severe panic attack, right in the middle of paradise. This was what I'd been so afraid of. In order to cope, I could not speak, except for a few whispered words.

"Lie down with me. Hold my hand."

I felt claustrophobic from the heat. There was no air conditioning at the resort. Would I need to be airlifted back to Tahiti? Then what? I stared up at the ceiling without uttering a single word. A full hour passed before the attack subsided. It left me feeling fragile and not in control of my own mind. I felt relieved when I returned to normalcy, but how long would it be until the next one, and how far was the shadow of terror going to pull me down?

The next day we heard about a tourist at our hotel who had an appendicitis attack and had to be helicoptered out. It was odd: I had so clearly imagined that it would be me. A hut over the water became available. This was the epitome of living. To enter the water for a swim, all we had to do was descend a few stairs. When we returned, we could rinse off under the outdoor shower and then take those few stairs back up to our hut. I have a picture of Jerry luxuriating under that outdoor shower.

We met two other couples with whom we spent some time. We had them over for drinks one afternoon and watched a manta ray put on a show for us right beneath our patio. I wore an ankle-length pink-and-white-flowered pareo I had bought that day. A pink and white lei of fresh orchids was awaiting me on the doorknob to our hut from the management. That night I looked very coordinated in my outfit, which was basically next to nothing: the pareo (a long wrap, tied in the front with a slit up the middle), no bra, just panties, flip-flops, and lei. That became my favorite way to dress for the rest of the time we were there.

I didn't experience another panic attack, and despite the one I had, Bora Bora remained one of my favorite trips. But it was a reminder that I could not feel confident in my ability to live free of confining mental problems, and I didn't like it one bit. I wanted to know I could stand on my own two feet.

Robby – 2012

Christmas was approaching and I had not had a lover since Brad, if you could call what we did lovemaking. That had been many months ago and I needed a lover, one who could perform. For someone who wanted sex as much as I did, it was almost unfathomable to me that I wasn't having any.

As time went on I realized I was now free to enjoy sex in any way I chose, and I was eager to play out my newly-found freedom with a man in real life.

So I went back to the building blocks - internet dating sites, not sex sites.

There was a new man who appealed to me on Plenty of Fish. He said he was fifty-eight. He responded right away. He wrote that he was a touchy-feely person and that sex was very important to him; I wrote back it was important to me, too.

We met at … you guessed it … El Torito. I wondered

if the bartender would recognize me. I had been apprehensive on the way over. I had dated a few men but they fell flat, like the guy who took me to Acapulco's for dinner and later asked me for the money he'd spent on dinner because I didn't want to see him again. Was this going to be another forgettable date?

The minute I laid eyes on Robby I was attracted to him. Was it mutual?

We took a table and he sat opposite me, but asked, "Would you like to sit across from each other or side by side?" Then I knew.

My answer: "Side by side."

As we drank Cadillac margaritas and ate, we flirted madly, but he didn't touch me.

I think it was sometime after our second margarita that I whispered in his ear, "For someone who is supposed to be touchy-feely, you're not very touchy-feely."

This wasn't terribly clever, but I wanted to kiss him and I couldn't think of anything else to say. He kissed me. He wasn't as good a kisser as Larry or Brad, but I was wildly attracted to him, enjoyed his company, and I wanted more. Our hands were all over each other. Would I take him home with me?

That was a big question. I prefer to wait until I know someone a little better, but every time I'd pass up the opportunity on the first date, it was like pulling teeth to get a second. After three margaritas and dinner, Robby and I left, said goodnight, and went to our respective cars. I turned the key to start the engine and then stopped. There was no question I wanted to have sex with him. I asked myself what I waiting for, picturing the letdown of going home alone.

I abruptly climbed out of my car, went to his, and in fits and starts asked him why he hadn't pursued coming home with me and did he prefer to wait until the next time, but before I could complete my sentence, he said, "I'd love to." And so I took him home.

Robby had a spectacular body. He was firm like an athlete. He worked out and ran daily. We had kissed so much in the restaurant, I think both of us were ready to move to the next step. When we got into bed, he immediately gave me oral sex.

"You taste soooo good," he said, in a booming voice and with tremendous enthusiasm.

That got me even more turned on. I was glad I could arouse such a high level of excitation. I remembered Brad and his prematurely ejaculating. My connection with Robby was stronger and more passionate; I had the sense that this time would be different.

He pressed his tongue between my legs, moaning, reveling in the moment, and so was I. He didn't continue long enough for me to have a chance at having a climax, but I was eager to feel his hard cock inside me. I knew it could take time to become fully in sync sexually, to know how to heighten the experience for the other. I was not so concerned about having an orgasm; I wanted him to fuck me. It had been so long.

But Robby also couldn't perform. He blamed it on the

liquor. He asked for water, hoping that would improve the situation. It didn't. Finally, I took his flaccid cock in my mouth and though Robby never got hard, he came. I never knew this was possible before. His expression of release was loud and fantastic.

He ran his fingers lightly across my body. The feel of the human touch was something I'd been missing for too long. He asked me to lie on top of him, and as I felt his powerful body beneath me, I remembered how revitalizing and reaffirming it was to be close to a man again.

I cared that he couldn't penetrate me, but it didn't stop me from wanting to see him again. There was a lot of affection between us, and I felt hopeful I'd hear from him.

Robby didn't spent the night, which was fine with me, even a relief. My apartment was small and it took the pressure off me to entertain him. It's not like he could perform so we'd most likely not have sex again. When I called Lisa to tell her what a great time I'd had, she said she thought it was a bad sign that he didn't stay and that whomever she'd been with had always stayed with her. That was difficult to hear and caused me to wonder if she was right.

Robby said he would call me the following week. I didn't feel concerned at the time he said it, but the next day, it suddenly seemed like a long time away. Still, I'd hoped it would be worth the wait. I liked him a lot. I hoped like crazy he would call.

The thought crossed my mind more than once how nice it would be to have a date for New Year's Eve. I

warned myself not to get my hopes up. I knew they could
so easily be dashed. But it would be nice, I allowed.

I had met Robby on a Wednesday. By Sunday, I was
beginning to feel disconcerted when I saw that he was
online but not calling me. And then I received an email
from him saying that over the weekend he had met
someone who lived a block away, and that it would be
easier to get to know somebody who lived close. Did I
believe it? No, because he was online three times that day.
And he only lived in Costa Mesa, twenty minutes away.

Some months later I saw him online again and re-read
his profile. I noticed he confessed in the body of the profile
to being sixty-eight, while the top of the profile read fifty-
eight. For fifty-eight, he was a jock; for sixty-eight, he was
phenomenal.

I thought a lot about Robby. I didn't know how long it
was going to take me to get over this one, but having this
disappointment come during the holidays made it worse. I
had difficulty letting it go. Thoughts of calling him
permeated my mind right before thoughts rejecting the
idea. Then I called him. I knew the only way to do it was
if I could be funny. I had told him previously that I was
writing a memoir.

He answered right away, sounding out of breath.

"You out for a run?" I asked.

"Yes."

"I just have one question."

"Okay," he answered.

"How can I put you in my memoir if I see you only

one time?"

He laughed. That's exactly what I wanted to have happen. But then he just rambled on about meeting someone close to where he lived whom he could get to know more easily, and that he was dating several women, a contradiction to his email where he wrote that he had met one woman, and it went downhill from there.

And so it ended—not horribly, but not the way I wanted. And here he is in my memoir anyway!

A thought came to me over the next several days that I wished I could have said to him. *But you came in my mouth! Doesn't that count for something?*

Hank – 2012

After I licked my wounds over Robby, I went back to Benaughty.com. Yes, I'd rather have had an in-person relationship, but I still had needs and I was receiving some satisfaction online.

I thought it would be impossible to find anyone sexier than Rod; and then I met Hank. Our emails were flying back and forth over the next three months. Then one day he wrote that he was getting off the site and offered his phone number if I'd like to talk. Did I really want to try phone sex again? Those few moments with Rod had been so awkward. I thought about it for several days and then one night I did call him. Hank had a deep, sexy voice. He guided me with the way he was talking to me. He led the way and I followed. Phone sex came naturally to me with Hank.

The more we talked, the sexier it became.

"I'd be honored to give you my best, making you

climb walls, driving you insane while bringing you to the edge of orgasm, then pulling you back to the edge again while looking you in the eye. Running my tongue over your hyper-sensitive clit, it's that one slow lick that makes you explode. My tongue ... my hands ... my lips ... my balls ... my cock made to serve you and your every dirty, naughty, sexual, multi-orgasmic desire. Come to Reno to get it."

I confided to him that I'd had a fabulous orgasm thinking of him and his words. The photo he put up on Benaughty.com was only a partial body shot, and although I wanted to see his face, he was already having an impact on me.

He replied, "You've needed a cum like this for a long time. You know who to come to."

I wanted to head for Reno on the next plane out of Long Beach.

"I'm missing you in my mouth. I want to be down between your thighs waking every nerve, making you beg for more.

"You know who you need to take you on the great journey of the ultimate orgasm. Anybody can fuck your pussy, tits, ass, I'm fucking your mind. Pure freedom, only accessible with me, to reach the ultimate cum because you know I care. We'll get to the place where we can reach each other's thoughts.

"Keep in mind my cock is waiting to ruin you for any other man. I'll wrap my lips over your swollen clit making you pray for the cum, making you feel like a real woman.

I'll give you all the cock you can handle. Come get it. It's here and ready for you."

I loved to hear this guy talk!

"Wish you were here to see how hard you make me. Climb up on me, baby and straddle my face. I'll be licking you, sucking you as you fuck my face, giving you all the time you need, letting me drive you insane."

The way he was talking *was* driving me insane! I never heard anyone talk like this.

"No rush. No rules. Rain down on me. Then when you cum I'll go down and lick you clean."

It wasn't long before we started asking about each other. It always led to sex, but we grew into friends. Sometimes we'd just talk about what was happening in our lives. But when I orgasmed with Hank during phone sex, it was extremely satisfying.

Hank liked to push me to the edge. He wrote me that I needed more than one lover … at the same time. I had fantasized about being with more than one man before. Hank had a brother. They'd done it before. Two men, one woman. He mentioned to me what a big cock his brother had, just like his, only thicker. I had used that fantasy to have more than one memorable orgasm.

Could I ever do it? I would have to feel extremely safe, and I didn't know if I would ever feel that safe. To trust that much … I doubted it. And right then, I would have been happy to find just one man who wanted to be with me and could sustain an erection!

Something new was happening to me. I was finding

my parent's negative sexual messages had slipped away, and I realized if I didn't have to hold onto their sexual messages, then I didn't have to hold onto their negative emotional messages either. I was giddy with joy!

Alex – 2012

Alex and I met on Benaughty.com and began sending each other highly sexual emails several times a day. I was enjoying it. He said he wanted to meet me and have a real relationship. He was very persuasive, and his intense interest in me fed a deep need to be physically intimate with someone. He had been working in Las Vegas as an engineer for the army, and when he arrived home in Virginia, he sent me an email.

> Hi, Baby,
> All rested up. Just got back from the office. Getting my things in order. Hope your day is going well. I have missed you and wish you were here. I would love to be fingering your clit and pussy as you lick and swallow my cock and balls. I bet you could fit most of it in your throat sucking it hard. I will make you cum many times. You will love it.

Your man,
Alex

He lived across the country. It seemed so impractical
that anything could come of a relationship with him. But
he was very strong in his pursuit.

In prior emails, he'd told me he was going to
Afghanistan soon to work on army planes over there. I
didn't feel right leading him on when I knew I could never
be with him because of our age difference, and his lack of
knowledge about my real age. I tried to talk him out of
continuing to think of me.

Hi Alex,
I could exchange sexy emails all day long and not tire
of it, but you want more. I told you I'd made up my
mind when I came to this site that I would never meet
anyone on it. I still feel the same.

I want you to know that this has absolutely nothing to
do with you and everything to do with me. I think
you're a terrific guy and some woman will be very
lucky to have you in her life.

Even if we were to get together and really hit it off, it
is very unlikely I would be happy being back east.
I'm a California girl. I love the weather in L.A., and
the easy lifestyle suits me. This is not good-bye from

my perspective, but it might be from yours, and I understand if it is. It is with great reluctance that I write this, but I don't think it's fair to you to lead you to think there would be more.

Lynn

Had I been the same age as Alex, I would've jumped at the chance to meet him, and though it is probably true that I would be unhappy back east, it is possible that I might have acclimated myself and enjoyed it. He felt we were so right for each other, and maybe sexually we were, but I was so much older and I couldn't bring myself to confess that. If I had, and if he became angry, I would feel very badly. Also, if he reported me to the site—well, I wasn't ready to be thrown off because I was still enjoying it. It was a very fertile source...for my mind, body, and book.

I had that fantasy again that if I told him the truth, perhaps, just perhaps, he would have said, "I don't care, I want you anyway." I wasn't sure what was worse, playing out the fantasy and taking the chance he would be infuriated with me, or handling it the way I did and wondering what might have been. I knew if someone lied to me by twenty-five years I'd be very angry.

But Alex wouldn't give up. And so I finally told him the truth, and waited. Waited for his rage. Instead, he confessed that he had lied too! He was fifty-four rather than forty-eight! So it made the difference fifteen years, instead of twenty or more. And besides, he said, our age difference didn't bother him. And that's what I'd hoped to hear.

Our conversations continued, and so did his efforts to meet me. He was due to go to Afghanistan for three months. He had one more weekend before he would deploy. He invited me to come to Virginia. I said I would think about it. Alex sent me another email.

We need to meet. I am very happy we have been expressing our feelings and it is beautiful, nothing to be ashamed of. We are human. We are born, grow up and develop our urges and traits and go on our way through life and we share our feelings. I am very sexual and I know you are too. It's been a long time for me ... five years now. I need to make love and if I am going to make love, I want it to be with you. I am well paid and can afford to travel and will fly you anywhere so we can be together. Please let's give this a chance. I know we can make it happen. I'll give you one kiss for each of the stars in the night sky and a hug like you have never experienced."

Some people might call that corny. I thought it was endearing. I wanted those kisses. I wanted that hug.

Year Nine – 1990

Nine years of marriage were uneventful. Jerry and I were often very stressed for money and had some major arguments about it, but most of the time we enjoyed our lives together.

Thanksgiving was approaching, and the Sunday before, we were invited to Jerry's son's home in Redlands, California. Gabe and his then wife, Marcia, were preparing a barbeque. We helped ourselves at the buffet table and went outside to eat at a wooden picnic table. I took a seat at the end of the table and Jerry sat to my right. I took a forkful of salad and then I noticed *it*. On Jerry's left arm, about two inches above his elbow, I saw something that chilled me to the bone: several large bumps, purple, black, and blue.

"What is that?" I asked Jerry.

"I don't know."

"How long has it been there?"

"About six months," he answered.

"Six months? Why did you ignore it?"

He gave me an answer, but I was in such shock so I don't remember what it was. Jerry had often ignored important things, choosing to drive on threadbare tires, averting his glance from the malignant growth on his arm, and not once during our infrequent coupling did he question whether I had achieved orgasm. Both of us paid dearly for his shortcomings.

The why was irrelevant at this point since we couldn't go back, and I had never been so angry with him. The other things he had ignored were fixable. This was not.

I questioned myself as to how I had never noticed it, or even touched it by accident, but I hadn't. And that too, didn't matter now.

"You'd better get yourself to a doctor immediately," I warned. It was not a sweet tone I used. I didn't know what it was, but it looked lethal. It was so disturbing to me that Jerry had let it go for six months that I promptly banished it from my mind.

The next afternoon I was in the kitchen, trying to figure out what to make for dinner, when the phone rang.

"Hi, it's me," Jerry said. "I'm at the doctor's."

And then it came back to me. The bumps. The doctor.

"He thinks I have melanoma, and that it's Stage IV. There is no Stage V."

My anger dissipated, and I became bent on a mission to save Jerry's life. One of my parent's best friends had died of melanoma just nineteen months after diagnosis. I knew it could be deadly. I called doctors, hospitals, anyplace I could glean information to help Jerry.

I went with Jerry to his dermatologist. A date was set for him to go into the hospital and have the lesions removed. The day after surgery the diagnosis was confirmed: malignant melanoma, lymph nodes invaded. I knew instantly this would take Jerry's life, but I didn't know when or how much suffering he might have to go through before it did.

No treatment was recommended for Stage IV malignant melanoma at that time. Some patients chose chemotherapy, but there was no proof that it helped extend or save a life. One of the doctors felt it could actually do harm, weakening the body's immune system so that the good cells were less able to fight the bad. I labored over the decision, but Jerry didn't. He decided he would not seek chemotherapy. If things changed in the future, he'd reevaluate. I didn't know which was the right decision and was glad he was the one to call it. What if I had chosen to go, or not to go, with chemo and the outcome turned out poorly? I would never have forgiven myself.

~

I had lived in Marina del Rey from the time I was twenty-seven and through nine years of marriage to Jerry. I loved it; the weather, the water, the boats. I wanted to live there the rest of my life. But Jerry's business was struggling. We were barely making it. I had been working writing screenplays, but earning no money. And now he was ill.

He finally had to tell his family, both about the cancer and our financial condition. They were generous and we were lucky to have them in our lives. They agreed to help us out, but wanted us to move from the Marina into one of their apartment buildings which, coincidentally, was close to Cedars Sinai Hospital, where Jerry would seek treatment.

The cancer forced us to change our lives. Jerry had to give up his business, which was very tough on him. I, along with Jerry, had to give up living in the Marina.

Reprieve to Apocalypse – 1993

I became a mother hen. If any friend had the slightest cold, I cancelled plans we had made. I had to protect Jerry every way I could.

Three years passed without incident. With a diagnosis of Stage IV malignant melanoma, this was very unusual. Jerry was still playing tennis and working, although now he was functioning as a building manager to his brothers' building in which we lived, rather than as a real estate developer.

While I was doing research for Jerry, I noticed that my hips and knees were starting to ache and that walking and sleeping were painful. I had X-rays taken, and they showed that I had a severe case of osteoarthritis. I had inherited this from my father, who had both hips and one knee replaced. An orthopedic surgeon said it might be worthwhile for me to have a meniscus surgery. It was a relatively minor surgery and might postpone the need to have a full knee replacement for six months. With Jerry doing so well, I made an appointment for the procedure.

∼

Jerry had his quarterly MRI. As usual, I went with him to see his oncologist for the results.

I hated Cedar's patient rooms; they were so small that Jerry and I could not sit together. I wanted to be able to hold Jerry's hand, which was impossible. So Jerry sat on a chair at one end of the examination table and I sat at the opposite end. The doctor put up the X-ray.

We weren't prepared. We didn't expect it. Why should we? Everything was going fine. And then it wasn't.

"Jerry's melanoma has spread to his brain."

"What?" I shouted, stunned.

But it wasn't "Jerry's melanoma." He didn't ask for it. Make it somebody else's melanoma. I immediately cancelled my surgery and we went to the surgeon's office to book Jerry's.

Jerry's sisters and brothers, his daughter, Darlene, and my Dad and Lee were at the hospital while Jerry had the surgery to remove the tumor from his brain. Surprisingly for how serious the surgery was, it only lasted two hours.

Throughout his entire ordeal, from his diagnosis onward, Jerry never once complained. That was heroism to me. I had great admiration for him. I knew I could never be that brave.

At this point we made the decision to try chemotherapy. Now we had to try anything and everything. I continued my research and located a doctor back east who had a chemotherapy drug that was being tested in trials in France to specifically help patients whose melanoma had gone to the brain. I called him. He agreed to send the drug to our doctor. This felt like a tremendous victory. Jerry and I celebrated our birthdays, my fifty-first, his sixty-first with a sense of hopefulness.

A New Day – 1996

Two and a half years had passed, and while the chemo
hit Jerry hard and made him extremely fatigued and
irritable, he was still alive. Our lives were very restricted
but we had to accept it. What else could we do?

I had gone to the market to pick up a few things, and as
I entered the lobby of our apartment building I couldn't
know my life would change in a totally different way.

I saw a puppy, but not just any puppy. This creature
jumped straight up in the air when called. This puppy had
a real personality, and you could tell he was smart. I was
completely taken with it.

"What is it?" I asked.

"Wheaten Terrier."

When I finally tore myself away and got upstairs, I told
Jerry about it. He had wanted an animal for a long time,
but every building in which we'd lived had refused to have
dogs. And I didn't want a cat. His brothers owned our

building, and they too were adamant: No dogs!

But I couldn't get this puppy off my mind. I became as impassioned about the puppy as I had about finding a cure for Jerry. By this time, we were restricted in what we could do in our lives. Jerry was numbed mentally, and exhausted physically, from the treatments. If we could have a puppy we wouldn't have to go out for entertainment. We could stay at home and enjoy our own little four-legged entertainment center.

I called Ruth, Bill's wife. I knew if I had a chance, she would be the one I'd need to sell the idea to. I told her I thought it might help Jerry and me, give us both a light in the tunnel, even if we didn't know where that tunnel would take us.

"I'll talk to Bill," she said.

To their credit, Bill and Jack broke their rules. We could have a puppy! A trainer I spoke to coined Wheatens "clowns with wings on their feet." We needed something to be happy about, and a clown with wings on his feet would do it.

It was a challenge to find a breeder with Wheaten puppies, but I finally located one with four-week-old pups. She told me I was welcome to come see them, but I wouldn't be able to pick one because they had to see which ones would qualify to be show dogs.

I went. I saw. I didn't conquer. It only took a few seconds to fall in love. The little boy with the turquoise ribbon came right up to me and licked my finger continually until the breeder finally took him away and put him back in his crate with his mother, two brothers, and three sisters. I knew I was in the right place, because it was the exact make-up of Jerry's family: three brothers and three sisters.

The breeder told me I could come back to see him again and I did. The next visit she told me the same thing.

"I can't come back again," I said. "I'm getting attached to him. Let me know when you've made a decision."

I knew having that puppy would raise our spirits. What I didn't know was if we'd be lucky enough to get him.

Zacky – March 1996

While I was waiting to hear about the puppy, I was
seeking a literary agent. I had been writing screenplays for
years and generated a number of ideas for television
dramas. I caught the interest of a few producers who
optioned some of my work, but I really needed the
assistance of an agent who had better access to the movers
and shakers than I did.

International Creative Management, a major talent
agency, read one of my screenplays and set up a meeting.
Although there was no contract, when we met they offered
an informal agreement, and a promise to make efforts on
my behalf.

I told Jerry and he was so happy for me. Then I
checked my answering machine for messages. There was
only one.

"We've decided you'd give the puppy a wonderful
home and—" I didn't need to hear anymore. I ran to the

living room where Jerry was seated and jumped up and down. "We got the puppy! We got the puppy!"

And joy came into our house. I named the puppy "Zacky." That's what I would have called a male child if I had ever had one. When we brought him home from the breeder's I weighed him on Jerry's scale. He weighed a whopping six pounds.

We threw a puppy party, inviting several friends over to celebrate the new addition to our family. Everyone brought presents for our little bundle of joy. Jerry and I finally had something to feel good about.

But about a week later, the puppy stirred up something in Jerry that concerned me. Jerry didn't have patience where Zacky was concerned, which was understandable. We had been taking turns looking after Zacky at night, but it was just too difficult for Jerry. And I began to notice that the puppy was depressed. I knew I had to do something. So after I spent some time with Jerry in the evening, I sat down on the floor with the puppy to spend time specifically engineered to raise his spirits. Zacky sat so close to me you couldn't have gotten a dog bone between us. I threw the ball. Sometimes he would actually go after it. I tickled and kissed him, and pretty soon he was a happy puppy again.

One day Jerry confessed he had hit Zacky when I wasn't home. This was deeply disturbing to me. I was glad he mentioned it though, so I could redouble my efforts to see that both Jerry and Zacky got what they needed.

But puppy and all, the pressure was impacting me. It had been nearly six years of dread over Jerry's health, terrified over what the next day might bring. I had to get away for the night. I had to feel what it meant to be outside such dire circumstances.

Jerry's daughter, Darlene, and his son, Neil, agreed to come over and spend the night and let me go away to a local hotel. I went to Shutters on the Beach in Santa Monica, a casual but elegant hotel on the water. It was just what I needed to restore myself.

I sat by the pool and gazed out at the ocean. Jerry and I had been to this hotel many times before and had happy memories here. We had breakfast in the coffee shop and sat right where I was sitting for a few hours, just to get a change of pace. At dinnertime, I had a meal at that same coffee shop. Fine dining was available in their restaurant, but I didn't want anything fancy. I just wanted to be surrounded by life. I watched vacationers, waiters, and the sun setting. It brought me a glimmer of hope, but for what I did not know.

I called Darlene the next morning and she told me two things: the puppy kept crying in his crate and after a few hours she and Neil needed some relief, so they let Zacky out and he slept on the floor with them and all was well there. And then she told me the other thing, Jerry fell.

Grief – July 1996

A new surgery called radiotherapy was to be performed on Jerry. A band of metal was secured around his head, and then he received treatment. The procedures were becoming more intense and more terrifying. What was happening to my poor husband?

It was the middle of June, and Jerry needed a hospital bed at home, which he did not want. But he simply could not cope outside of it. We were now on an irreversible path. We hired a nurse, but it wasn't long before I had to call hospice. Jerry did not receive comfort from them and in fact, railed against them. He did not want to die, and they were, understandably, a reminder of what was ahead for him. But I took comfort. In fact, I don't know what I would have done without them. I completely let go in the hospice woman's presence.

"I feel so guilty," I told her. "Some days I go down to the Marina and am gone for several hours." I had no forgiveness for myself, but she did.

"Many wives leave their husbands and never come back," she said. "They just can't take it. It's too devastating and they refuse to do it." I had never given a thought to leaving Jerry. I didn't know how I was going to get through it though. In the end, it would be day by day, hour by hour.

~

On July 1, 1996 Jerry died. I was with him and heard him stop breathing. I was glad I was there when he took his last breath. The clock read 10:12. I thought of all the TV shows I had seen where the doctor called time of death. This time I called it.

Jerry had lived six years from diagnosis to death. That was a long time for someone with Stage IV malignant melanoma. I didn't know if it was the drug we got from France or just luck, but whatever the reason, he outlived most other people with this disease. Strange, though, it just didn't seem to matter. In the end he lost his battle. Jerry was only sixty-three.

There was much to do. I called Jerry's son, Toby, and the funeral home, and Jerry's oncologist to let them know of Jerry's passing. The funeral home picked up Jerry. Darlene had stayed overnight and wanted to go to her home for a while. I didn't want to be alone, so we took Zacky and went to Darlene's.

It was a hot July afternoon. I swam in Darlene's pool. It felt good to be in the water. The exercise made me feel alive. Zacky was so excited to be somewhere different that he ran around the pool like a crazy dog and finally fell in. He loved the ocean but hated the pool and wanted out of it. When I picked him up he was so scared that his legs went stiff. I carried him to the steps as fast as I could and let him make his escape. I had only been at Darlene's a short while and was already missing home to receive calls and communicate with friends about Jerry's death. I asked her if we could please go back. We gave Zacky a quick bath and left.

Darlene stayed a few nights with me, and it was so helpful having her there. She was very loving toward me, and although she had just lost her father, she was still sensitive to my loss.

The funeral service was held at Hillside Memorial Park and Mortuary, the final resting home of the Rosenbergs. Only fifty-three and not knowing where my life would lead me, I elected not to buy a plot for myself. I wasn't even sure that I wanted to be buried at all. Cremation was on my mind, with my ashes dropped into the sea. The thought of being confined in a coffin underground didn't appeal to me at all. I had spent enough time in confinement.

The reception was held in our apartment. I dropped Zacky off at the breeder for a few days. All of Jerry's sisters and brothers and spouses came, except for Jack Rosenberg, Jerry's brother who had died of pancreatic cancer a year before. Friends came in from out of town to stay with me afterward.

But then, about a week later, came the first night I would be by myself. You'd think I would have been prepared. I knew, or was pretty sure, Jerry would die from this disease. But in truth, there is no way to prepare for the ending of a life. You don't imagine yourself with only the walls and the furniture to talk to. Faced with utter unforgiveable silence, I found myself standing in the kitchen, holding onto the counter, crying and begging and screaming for Jerry to come back to me, as if repeating the cry would result in his magically returning to life.

I called the last friend who'd been with me. She had just arrived home. "Do you want me to come back?" she asked.

"Please," I answered.

She returned for another night. But finally I had to face being alone.

Healing – 1996

Grief took hold of me and wouldn't let go. Efforts to distract myself failed. I cried all the time. In the mornings I would bring Zacky into bed with me to play with him, only my tears got in the way. Zacky licked them off my face. I was touched by how sensitive he was and grateful that he was part of my life. But I still walked around with a heavy heart.

A friend suggested a grief group. It was held in Beverly Hills, not far from where I lived, so I went. Twenty people made up the group, too many to have time to repair each individual soul. I wasn't happy with the limited attention, so I stopped going.

Then I heard about another group, at St. Troy's Hospital in Santa Monica. Nuns ran the hospital at the time. This was a small group of seven people. Always on time, I sat there watching the parade of strange-looking people enter: one woman in a biker's jacket, another who

talked nonstop before group even started, and a man who
didn't speak at all, just wiped away tears the whole time.
Perhaps I looked as strange to them. But at least they
looked authentic, not like the Beverly Hills contingent, who
looked interchangeable.

I didn't want to stay in this group either, and told that
to my therapist at the time. I didn't identify with any of
them, so how were they going to identify with me? She
encouraged me to go to another meeting before giving up.
I did, and gradually I could recognize the human element
coming out in each of these people. And I began to open
up about embarrassing feelings.

"I've had fantasies of crawling into the coffin with
Jerry," I said.

Several people spoke up and said that was nothing
compared to their thoughts and fantasies. That was such a
relief! I grew close to four of the seven people, and in the
spring, one of the women and I went on a European
vacation together and had a wonderful time. Traveling
with someone who was also grieving was a comfort.

Because of the insurance money Jerry left me, I was
able to return to my beloved Marina. I moved into what I
had hoped would be the last home I would ever have, at the
Marina City Club where Jerry and I met. I lived, for a time,
in paradise. My apartment was on the ninth floor
overlooking the marina and the ocean through floor-to-
ceiling windows. Laying down in bed, all it took was a
slight turn of the head, and the entire harbor was laid out
before me.

Zacky was a different dog in this apartment, full of the devil. He'd interact with the world outside our unit by leaning his forearms on a wooden slat of patio railing, poking his head through and barking out a greeting to passersby.

I took Zacky everywhere with me—long walks, dog parks, the bank, Neiman Marcus in Beverly Hills. He was a fixture at the car wash, the local Chinese restaurant where he laid at the door, head and front paws inside, body outside, the pet store, and front lawn of the Ritz-Carlton down the street from where we lived. He was my pal, my best friend, my confidante, my child. His antics caused me to erupt in laughter more than any comedian ever could.

I had trained Zacky not to sleep in the bed with me, having read in a dog training book that if you ever anticipate having a relationship, not to let the dog sleep in your bed. So that's what I did, and he never came up. One morning, after I finished the breakfast dishes, I looked around for him, calling his name. The apartment wasn't very big, so if he was missing he couldn't have gone far. Still, I couldn't find him.

I walked from room to room. There were only four rooms including the bathroom, so it didn't take long to survey the floor in each room. No Zacky. Then, in the bedroom, something made me look on top of the bed. There he was, head on my pillow exactly like mine had been, body off the pillow, like mine. He didn't move as I approached, but glanced warily in my direction with obvious concern as to what I would do, if I would scold him. I laughed, leaned over, and embraced him, telling him what a funny dog he was and how much I loved him.

The owners of the condo I was renting wanted to sell and I had enough money to buy it. Owning my own place for the first time in my life gave me great satisfaction. I thought if I met someone he could move in with me, or we could move to a larger condo in the same complex. But who was the someone I was going to meet? Would there even be a someone? And what would sex be like?

∽

For years, the deterioration of my hip and knee joints caused me pain walking and sleeping. Now it was affecting me while I was driving and even sitting. I remember driving home on the freeway, barely being able to keep my foot on the gas pedal because I was in such agony, afraid I wouldn't make it home even though I had less than a mile to go.

The surgeon told me I wouldn't feel better until I had all four joints replaced. One replacement wasn't going to bring me much relief. I had a dog to look after and no one to help me with food shopping and other necessities. I didn't know how I was going to manage. But gradually, things fell into place. I found a wonderful woman who took in dogs, and I hired a nurse for after the surgery, who would go shopping and look after me. Fortunately, my inheritance from Jerry made this possible.

I had seven major joint replacement surgeries while I lived in that condo: both knees, both hips, both shoulders, and a second replacement for one of the hips. I was often in acute pain and always seemed to be in recovery.

Arriving home from one of my surgeries, I met Don in the elevator, probably the worst time to introduce myself. But that's what I did. Don was tall and cute, and seemed to have a nice personality.

Once most of the surgeries were completed and I could walk without crutches, I signed up as a docent for The Getty Center museum. After six months, The Getty gave a party to thank the volunteers for the work we had done. I invited Don to the party.

He came to the condo to pick me up. I invited him in, and we sat on the sofa. Zacky came up to greet him, tail wagging at the speed of light, but Don didn't put a hand out to pet him, didn't even acknowledge him. Red flag! In my opinion, if a man likes a woman or vice versa, you should make some attempt to be friendly to your date's dog or cat. It's a mistake to assume it doesn't matter. It does matter!

I enjoyed Don's company and he held my hand during the party, but I put the brakes on quickly. Zacky was one issue; perhaps Don would grow friendlier toward him if he knew it was important to me. But there was the subject of finances. Don was an attorney, but he had no ambition. Being a go-getter myself, I knew I would be frustrated by a man who didn't care about money, didn't want to work hard to get it and the niceties money could buy. I wanted to

travel and I wanted to better myself. And although I didn't
need the moon, I did want some of the finer things in life,
so I held back. A relationship, therefore, never developed.
It did, though, for Don, when he met a woman from
Match.com. The last I heard they had moved in together.

Brad – 2012

I met Brad on Benaughty.com. We did not have any
sexy chat. Though I tried to distract him from getting
together, Brad was intent on meeting me. He was fifty-
four. I had to tell him the truth about my age.

"Age is only a number," he said. We made a date to
meet at El Torito, where I had met Larry so long ago.

We sat at the bar and ordered margaritas. I again
ordered the "Cadillac" margarita, which comes with a shot
of Grand Marnier. I wanted a buzz. The predominant
thought on my mind was: How is Brad going to react to me
now that he's seeing me in person? Will my age be a turn-
off to him? From my point of view, Brad weighed more
than he had stated on his profile and he was shorter than he
touted, but did I even care?

Then, like Larry, he kissed me. And rubbed my back.
And suddenly it didn't seem to matter that he was ten or
more pounds overweight and was somewhere south of

5'10". His hand brushed my nipple. Oh! That got my attention.

We had another margarita. I felt his hand on my thigh. He moved closer to me, his body now touching mine. This time he slipped his hand in between my legs and pressed it upward on my clitoris. Reflectively, I placed my hand on the back of his neck and pulled him toward me, which enabled our mouths and tongues to work their magic again.

Now I was actually having a sexual interaction for real, not just a filler fantasy. Brad was a sensual man, and being touched by him felt good, very different from just chatting on Benaughty.com! Still, he was a complete stranger and I didn't feel comfortable taking him back to my apartment with me.

I arrived home, and found I couldn't stop thinking about him. I sent him an email.

"You got me extremely turned on. Enjoyed the evening. Hope you're thinking sexy thoughts of me."

Brad replied, "I am! You got me extremely hard. I wanted to take you right there in the parking lot. Love your breasts. Next time...Brad."

It took a week, but we finally got together. This time I invited him into my bed. Brad had an orgasm the moment he entered me. He muttered something about seeing me soon, as he left my apartment. I knew I would never hear from him again; but that was okay. Lesson learned: Sometimes the fantasy is better than the reality.

THE EROTIC ART SHOW – CIRCA 2012

A Short Story

It was just shortly before the chaos of the holidays when I received an invitation to an erotic art show. There was no charge but of course they'd be trying to sell their works of art. I don't know how they got my name; perhaps off of another gallery's list. Living in Los Angeles, I enjoyed visiting the local galleries from time to time and they'd always ask you to sign up if you wanted to be on a mailing list. Still, I had never been to anything like this before but I was intrigued by the idea and thought my boyfriend, Josh, might be too.

We had only been dating for three months but we were hitting our mid-forties, experienced with what we didn't want, and very drawn to each other. I had started to think this might be the real thing. I was

like an oasis in the desert for Josh whose ex-wife
hadn't wanted sex. Since sex was on my mind the
better part of every day, Josh's starvation was an
elixir to me. I had been married too, but my divorce
was years ago. The sex had been good once, but
ceased when we stopped caring to please each other.
Until I met Josh, my love life as a single woman had
been unpredictable and infrequent. But now we were
finally getting what we needed and could barely keep
our hands off each other.

When we went out for dinner that night I showed
him the invitation and asked him if he would like to
go.

"Sure," he said with gusto. "Naked women? I'll
go anywhere to see them."

I shook my head at him and smiled. "Not in the
flesh, baby, on the walls."

"Like I said, I'll go anywhere to see them."

On the night of the event we tossed ideas back
and forth on what constituted appropriate dress for
this kind of occasion. We had thus far been very
open with each other about sex, but we weren't going
to this to have sex, but to view it. We decided on
conservative attire to be on the safe side. Josh wore a
navy jacket and gray slacks, and I slipped on a mid-
thigh black silk dress. Other than some thigh
exposure, I was totally covered up. The invite said
there would be champagne and food so we didn't
need to concern ourselves with eating before we

went.

We pulled up to the gallery and a valet took our car. It was impossible to tell from the brick and glass exterior what to expect inside. A bouncer opened the door for us and upon entering we were immediately offered flutes of fine champagne, Veuve Clicquot in fact. They weren't sparing any expense. The main gallery was filled with lively people milling about. Everyone seemed to be talking about the paintings.

Josh took my hand and led me to the first painting, a watercolor which portrayed men and women giving each other oral sex. I stood open-mouthed. Josh and I hadn't had a chance to discuss our reaction to what we were seeing before we were offered a second glass of champagne. By now I was feeling a little tipsy and suddenly very aroused.

When I stepped in front of Josh, he embraced me and kissed my neck. As I leaned back into him I could feel his erection. His rock-hard cock was pressing into my butt. It was clear we were feeling the effects of this art show and the champagne. In spite of being in the presence of other people, I inadvertently let out a sigh. Eyes began to focus in our direction so we detached from one another and moved along to see some of the other art.

The other paintings were even more captivating: a furtive glance here, a touch of a woman's nipple there. I didn't know if it was the champagne, or the art, or both but I was beginning to feel a little unsteady on my feet.

"I think I need to sit down."

Josh took my hand again and we looked around for a chair. There wasn't one.

"C'mon," he said, leading me down a hallway to a door. He opened it and we entered. It held janitor supplies, a sink, and now us. And there was a chair. I sat down. A few minutes passed and he asked me how I was feeling.

"Better. We can go back out there now," I answered. I rose out of the chair.

"No. Not yet," he said, closing the door.

He cradled the palm of his hand up against my mound and pressed firmly. I gasped. Then he sank to his knees and tugged on my panties. When they were separated from my crotch, he blew hot air on my pussy. I immediately thrust my pelvis toward his face while pulling his head toward me.

It crossed my mind that someone may find us or hear us, which would be embarrassing to say the least. But I couldn't stop now. Josh's lips were wrapped around my clit and there was nothing I could do but relish it, nothing I was going to do but let him savor me. Unlike some guys, Josh really dug oral sex, telling me over and over how he loved my aroma, and how one taste would drive him wild. He never failed to bring me to orgasm, not once.

I was on the verge of cumming and the urge to moan was great. I tried to stifle it but the sensation of being so close was getting the better of me.

"Oh! Just make me cum, Josh, that's all I want, baby, suck it out of me!" I said too loudly. Someone was sure to overhear. He knew I was close and he just kept on until, "Oh! Oh! Oh!" I couldn't stop myself from crying out and finally I came all over his tongue and mouth. Even after I climaxed, I needed to have his lips on me a few moments more to completely finish me off.

"That was so good," I told him. "Now it's your turn."

"I don't know. You know how loud I am."

I looked down and saw his erect penis tenting his pants. "I know but I can't leave you like this." I quickly unzipped his trousers, reached inside and caressed that hard cock, now tipped with precum. It felt swollen, about ready to burst, and there was no question it was in need of my mouth grasping tightly around it. I squatted down and took his shaft deep into my throat. He let out a guttural cry that I thought was sure to give us away. *So damn it, we'd be found out. Who the hell cares?* What mattered was this moment, and nothing was going to stop me from giving Josh the powerful ejaculation I knew would cum.

Just then I heard live music coming from the gallery. It was a relief because I knew Josh would shoot his load any minute. I stroked his member steadily with one hand and ran my fingernails gently over his balls with the other. But the last thing I would do, the thing I knew he couldn't resist no matter what, was insert a finger in his ass. One finger was all it took.

"My God, oh God, suck me off, baby!" And that was it. His hot, thick cum shot down my throat and all over my face and mouth and he just kept coming. I didn't know if he would ever stop, nor did I care.

It took us a few minutes to calm down and regain our equilibrium. We both straightened ourselves up. I pulled up my panties and Josh zipped his slacks. We washed up in the sink and, when we felt somewhat together, we returned to join the other guests.

We were offered a third glass of champagne which we accepted. "This is my last," Josh said.

"Mine, too," I responded. "I'm starved, let's get some food."

We were impressed by what appeared before us on the buffet table; the delicacies ranged from shrimp to caviar. After we ate, we took in more paintings in yet another room off the main gallery. One of the hostesses came up to us and asked if we were enjoying the show. We nodded, "Oh, very much."

"You might enjoy our game room," she offered.

"We'll check it out," Josh responded.

"It's right through there," she said, pointing to a corridor.

"Shall we?" Josh held out his hand to me. I

loved that he was affectionate.

The small sign on the door read "Game Room" so we knew we were at the right place.

"Wow!" I exclaimed, as we entered. "Maybe we were overheard. Maybe that's why we were invited to this little hideaway."

This was no ordinary game room. People were in various states of undress and having sex in a variety of ways, and there was lots of laughter and conversation. There was a woman with another woman, a man with two women, and couples engaging with other couples. There were several sofas, a double bed in the center of the room, and murals on the walls of couples fornicating. Wall sconces cast a dim light over the whole scene.

"Should we leave?" I asked Josh. "After all, we just had our own fun and games down the hall."

Just then a naked, well-hung young man, perhaps in his late twenties, and boyish-looking, came up to us. He spoke to Josh. "Do you mind if I enjoy your fine lady for a bit?"

"Well, it's okay with me, but you'd better ask her," Josh replied.

The young man looked at me. "Would you like to join me?"

We had never done anything like this before, but I had to admit to myself, the guy was very appealing: day-old scruff, spiky blond hair, and a nice musk-based aftershave.

"Are you sure?" I asked Josh, wondering if I myself was certain.

"I'll mingle," he nodded. "Don't worry about me."

I followed the young man to a sofa in the corner of the room. He slid a hand under my dress and, not taking his eyes off mine, circled my clit through the damp fabric of my panties. I was surprised I could get aroused so quickly—again. I glanced over at the spot where I left Josh and could see he was watching us. I wondered if he was upset, but he just smiled.

I reached my hand down to stroke the young man's cock. Just a brief touch sent me reeling. He was a solid eight inches and the girth was impressive. I dared to imagine what it might feel like to have it inside me. And then he slipped his fingers beneath my panties. It was just his fingers on my clit, nothing separating us now.

I threw my head back and whispered loudly enough for him to hear, "So good!" The boy was young but he knew what he was doing. I knew there were other couples nearby, there must have been half dozen or more around me, but I didn't care. This man had the touch. We began to kiss passionately but after a few minutes, he repositioned himself so that he was licking my clit and I was sucking his engorged cock.

We stopped to catch our breath for a moment and I saw Josh standing there.

"Mind if I join you?" he asked.

This would be something new. Perhaps dangerously new. Two men? How far did I really want to go? Would the boundaries ever go back the way they were if I did this? How would this impact my relationship with Josh? But I couldn't say no to Josh, couldn't hurt his feelings. I had to take the chance.

"Yes, please do," the young man and I answered simultaneously.

Just then a set of couples removed themselves from the bed. The three of us quickly made claim on it.

Josh removed his pants revealing an erect stalk, precum dripping from his slit. The young man withdrew from my pussy and in a sudden, very unexpected move, turned his head and began lapping up the moisture glistening from Josh's bulbous head! We were both a little stunned. Then the boy suckled the tip. I wasn't even being touched but I let out a cry. My heart was pounding. I never dreamed I could have been turned on by one man fellating another. I wondered what Josh was thinking. To my knowledge, he had never been with another man before. The boy finally withdrew and started nibbling on my nipple through the thin fabric of my dress. Josh thrust his hard cock into my cunt and started fucking me like never before. Somehow he was able to whisper that he'd never seen me so excited. That made me moan louder. Two men was evidently the ticket for me, something I had only fantasized about but never thought I'd experience.

Then Josh instructed the young man put his dick into my mouth which he did. I was so turned on I wondered if I would cum too soon.

"I want you to taste his cum shooting down your throat," Josh said to me.

The boy seemed to hesitate. I pulled away from the young man's shaft and urged him on. "You heard what he said," I commanded, then opening my mouth wide to him.

This sent the young man over the edge and he exploded in my mouth. Josh and I came an instant later.

We all just lay there for a few minutes trying to regroup. The crowd began to thin out. The three of us got dressed, and thanked each other for an incredible evening and headed home, tired and spent. This was an evening I may never duplicate, but one that I would never forget.

Alex Continued – 2012

Alex and I continued talking on the phone and exchanging emails. He told me he was 6′2″, 190 pounds. He sent me pictures and I liked his looks. He lived in Virginia, had been divorced for ten years, and had two daughters, one seventeen and the other nineteen.

Our emails and phone conversations continued to be very sexual, but in addition to that, he began to use terms of endearment, calling me "sweetie," and "my girl," and other affectionate terms. For several weeks I didn't let it affect me.

I kept telling him, "You don't know me...you don't know someone until you meet them."

This was the mantra my therapist used in terms of online dating, and I used it with Alex. That's why I kept trying to find a relationship locally.

At the end of seven weeks I let myself feel encouraged by what Alex was telling me. He told me he hadn't expected to fall so fast, but that I was the first woman in a long time with whom he felt a connection.

Again, he invited me to come to visit him in Virginia over the upcoming weekend before he deployed to Afghanistan to work on army planes. Suddenly this felt real, and personal. I started believing what he was telling me. I began to care about him and about what was happening between us. I thought seriously about meeting him in Virginia, but decided since I didn't know him that it would be less risky for him to come to Los Angeles.

"What would you think of coming here?" I asked.

"I could do that," he replied.

I was excited. Being very attracted to the man in the pictures he sent me, I anticipated great sex. One thing that concerned me was the fact that Alex's life experiences were limited. He barely read at all. He hadn't traveled for pleasure, only to the third world countries the military sent him to, like Uganda and Somalia. I had no idea what we would talk about, but I started thinking that maybe a sexual attraction was enough to start with. I needed and wanted good sex, and I was about to have it. Maybe good, if not great, sex with someone who cared about me was more than enough.

I did not hear from Alex the Wednesday or Thursday before the weekend. Friday morning I awakened to both my telephone and internet not working. I called Alex on my cell to inform him and to give him my cell number so he could reach me with the specifics of his trip.

I asked him when he was planning on coming in.

He said, "On Saturday."

I said, "Oh, I thought you were going to come in today."

And he answered, "I'll have to ask my boss if I can do that."

This sounded a little strange to me because I thought he was his own boss, except when he was managing his team of men who supposedly were already on their way to Afghanistan. But I didn't know for sure and I didn't want to appear demanding by pressing the point.

Friday felt like it was one hundred hours long. I didn't hear from Alex. By early evening I became concerned. I couldn't understand why he wasn't calling. Reluctantly, I called again, but this time his voicemail picked up. I asked him to call me and let me know when he was coming. I did not hear from him.

By Saturday I was very distressed. Something was wrong. I called him again, but he didn't pick up the phone or call me back. I emailed him, but didn't receive a response. Now I began to panic. What did it mean that I hadn't heard from him? *Isn't he coming? If not, why not?* I didn't know if it was something I said. I had asked him to meet me at an airport hotel rather than my picking him up at the airport. My therapist had suggested this in what I thought was an overabundance of caution. Alex had mentioned several times that the military gave him STD tests and that he hadn't had sex in five years. I asked him to bring the STD report. I apologized for asking him. He said it was okay and that he would do the same thing. I didn't know what he meant by "would." Would if he were a woman? Would if he were coming here? I never asked. Looking back, there were so many questions I didn't ask.

I emailed him a few more times and called him again, pleading with him that if I'd said something that upset him to please tell me what it was—that whatever it might have been, I hadn't done it deliberately, but that what he was doing was deliberate and very hurtful.

"If I were one of your daughters, and a man treated her this way, I would be very unhappy with that man." I tried everything, from every conceivable psychological, emotional, or intellectual angle that I could think of. I asked him, if nothing else, to please send me an email to let me know what had happened.

By Saturday night I was beside myself. Lisa and I had made plans to get together. I hadn't told her that I'd been regularly visiting a sex site, but at this point, I could no longer hold back that fact, judgments be damned. I told her everything. She was not judgmental.

Lisa asked me for his phone number and I gave it to her. I reiterated that he lived in Virginia. She asked for the area code. I gave it to her: "734."

"That's a Michigan number, not a Virginia number."

I was surprised, but didn't know whether it was an issue or not. Some people move, but keep their same cell number. I sent Alex one more email, asking him what the Michigan prefix meant, saying that he could still email me, that I would still appreciate knowing what had happened.

But I didn't hear back from him.

Even though "people who go on sex sites don't have feelings," mine were hurt. Men with whom I used to enjoy having "filler fantasy" sex didn't matter to me at all now. I had lost my enthusiasm for them, even Rod.

∾

A month passed, and I still thought about, and was baffled by Alex. I sent him one final email. I conveyed that I was not mad at him, not even sad, and said that if he had second thoughts, or just wanted to share with me what happened that I would appreciate it. It was a straightforward letter without emotion. I told him that for my part I thought I was too protective of myself and perhaps caused him confusion, in that when he asked what hotel he should stay in, I didn't even give him the name of a hotel. I think some part of me was afraid even to make that much of a commitment in case I didn't like him. He would have come all the way for nothing.

Much to my surprise, I received an email back from Alex. He explained that he was called to Afghanistan sooner than intended and that's why he didn't come out. He also said he did find some of the things I said confusing, but that they wouldn't have stopped him, that he had missed me and he, too, would like to see what we had.

We communicated for three weeks. There were spaces in between the times I wrote to him and when he wrote back. He told me that the internet was down much of the time in Afghanistan, and that he was working sixteen to eighteen hours a day. He apologized for not getting in touch with me sooner.

Unlike Lisa, I believed he was in Afghanistan. I still didn't understand why there was a house registered to him in Michigan. Lisa was a wizard on the computer and found things I could never find. Or why he didn't answer those initial phone calls. If he wanted to come to Los Angeles to meet me when he returned, I decided I would agree to it because at that point I was too curious not to do it. But I would be cautious and ask my questions, because many things just didn't make sense, and it bothered me that they didn't.

I didn't know why I had let this man get under my skin. Well actually, I did. I lacked attention, affection, and love, and I let myself be taken in by a man who seemed to care about me. My heart still skipped a little when I received an email from him. But I had to keep reminding myself to be careful because, as my therapist kept repeating, you don't know anyone until you meet them, and not even then until you've known them a while.

Though he apologized for leaving me hanging, I needed to understand how he could have been so cold to do that. And even though he'd said he was divorced, and that he had no reason to lie to anyone, I needed to understand why there was a house registered to his name with his email connected to it. It just didn't make sense, and with this, the glow on my enthusiasm faded a little. Sometimes I even agreed with Lisa that I shouldn't have given him the time of day.

I emailed a response back to Alex's last letter. Eight days passed, and there was no word from him. At least with Rod, I knew where I stood every single day.

Would I hear from him again? I had no idea.

Saying Goodbye – 1999

Three years after Jerry died, I lost my father. The intensity of his anger toward me had been so great I could only find the fortitude to visit him infrequently. One night Lee called me to let me know Dad was going into the hospital. Neither one of us had any expectations he would die. She told me he had written a letter to me in the event of his death, but that it was not nice and I should not read it.

I went out to the hospital. He said he had a stomachache and apologized for not being good company.

"You don't have to apologize for that," I said, meaning that there were other things I would like him to apologize for, but not feeling ill. But of course, I didn't spell it out like that, and his request for my forgiveness never came.

The next morning Lee called me to tell me Dad had died early that morning from heart failure. I listened to her and said little. I did not cry.

As with my mother, in spite of all the years and all the

tears, all the adoration and affection I had felt for him early in my life, at the news of his death I felt nothing. Like my mother, there was so much abuse and so much misery, so much of my life damaged, if not ruined, by his diminishment and condemnation of me, that I was devoid of feelings.

Thinking about it later, perhaps I felt a moment of regret for my inability to share my real feelings with either of my parents. But that was all. The insults, rampant criticism, and merciless undermining that drove me to protect myself by shutting down emotionally, and had caused me to be repressed sexually, would be no more. Releasing their indelible messages from inside my head would take a little longer.

I had invested a staggering amount of time, decades in fact, turning myself inside out, defiantly determined to win their love. I had refused to accept that it was an impossible goal, and that was my contribution to my own misery.

The questions still remained: Would I ever get beyond letting internal judgments from my parents debilitate me? Would I ever come to recognize that I was going down a path that wasn't good for me before I became embroiled in it? These were the questions I grappled with as my therapy continued.

Lee later castigated me for not shedding tears for my father. I secretly wondered how many she had shed. Lee and I were supposed to be friends. Dad had asked this of us, and we promised him that we would continue to remain close. He hadn't known, or wasn't willing to face, that Lee could be unpredictable and untrustworthy. I had seen it but believed that our friendship was solid.

Several months after Dad died I went with a girlfriend on an African safari. It was the most amazing trip of my life. When I returned I received a bizarre letter from Lee. It stated that she had gone to visit her sister down south, wherever down south was, and that she would contact me when she got back. She left no address or phone number as to where she could be reached, which I found very odd. I remembered I had the number of the manager of their condo building, so I called him and asked him if he had a location on Lee, as I would like to contact her.

"She's home," he said.

"No, I mean where did she go? She went to see her sister," I said, thinking he misunderstood me.

"She's home," he repeated. "I saw her this afternoon."

"You saw her this afternoon?" I said, incredulous. This was puzzling, to say the least. I pondered what to do. Finally I decided to call her, leaving a message on her voicemail asking her to please contact me, that friends and relatives were concerned about her, which they were. I also mentioned I didn't understand why she'd said she had gone down south when she was really at home.

Maybe I shouldn't have confronted her. Maybe I should have let her get in touch with me whenever she was ready. But after decades of holding back, this was one of the few times I let myself react.

The next and last thing I ever heard about Lee with regard to me was from friends and relatives. For reasons I will never understand, Lee had sent them and me, a seven-page letter criticizing me for everything she and my father perceived that I had ever done to them. The only reason I could conceive for her doing this was because her lie about going to see her sister was now uncovered and she didn't like it. Why she lied to begin with, I'll never know.

I could not bring myself to read the letter from my father so I asked my therapist to do it. It was familiar in its attacks on me. Because he read it, it took some of the sting out of it for me.

I never did find out whether or not the story Lee told about her husband and child, and the accident and fires were the truth.

September 11, 2001

Not long after having four major joint replacements, I realized I would have to seek out some way to earn an income other than working a secretarial job. Sitting all day was stressful to my joints. And I knew the insurance money Jerry left me wasn't going to last forever.

Two days before September 11, I decided to create a business making luxury umbrellas. I had recently been to France where I saw a potpourri of colorful and stylish umbrellas and I thought, *Why not have such great umbrellas in the U.S.?*

A neighbor gave me the phone number of a businessman friend of hers who imported electronic gadgets. Her thinking was that maybe he'd have some ideas to help me, which he did. Walt and I met for coffee, and he gave me a list of thirty-five umbrella factories in China for me to fax, inquiring about the styles of umbrellas they manufactured and their prices.

On September 11 at 6:30 in the morning I took Zacky for a walk. I encountered a woman speed walking, highly agitated and mumbling to herself, "They bombed the World Trade Center, they bombed the World Trade Center."

"What happened?" I asked, confused. I knew the World Trade Center had been bombed several years before, so why was she talking about that now?

As soon as we returned to the condo, I turned on the TV just in time to see the second building collapse. Then I understood why the woman was so distraught. I, along with millions of other people around the world, was glued to my television set.

I did nothing but watch TV for days afterward. Then, stepping out of my numbness, I realized this was no time to make luxury umbrellas. What would I do instead?

I called the businessman for suggestions and he came up with one. "Make American flag umbrellas. It would be patriotic and they should sell."

I thought it was a great idea and faxed the entire list of Chinese vendors to find a style I liked.

Responses began to come in, but I didn't see anything of interest until the very last one. The design was terrific. Walt said he would go in on it with me and that we should order 1,500 umbrellas, which we did. He'd been in the business of importing for so long that he didn't need a freight forwarder to assist him in importing the product. He did it himself, handling the flights and customs without a problem.

There was always the chance that once we received the

umbrellas they might not work. I had heard stories from friends and business acquaintances that many products exported from China didn't always function properly. But our flag umbrellas were perfect.

It was our agreement that Walt would handle the importation of the umbrellas, including shipping costs, and I would sell them. My sales experience consisted of selling myself as a singer and pianist to a number of hotels and restaurants over the course of my career; but selling a product was entirely different. Could I do it?

I decided to try a well-known drugstore in Beverly Hills, knowing they could afford to buy our product if they liked it. And they did. I sold two dozen umbrellas my first time out, which thrilled me to no end.

I kept making sales and enjoyed being my own boss again. Some of Mom and Dad's entrepreneurial skills had rubbed off on me. In two months I sold all 1,500.

Now I was left with a puzzle. What to do going forward? The effects of 9/11 were still strongly felt. Luxury umbrellas were out, but so were more flag umbrellas. The country was moving away from memorabilia of that tragic day.

I came across a fabric with sun protection built into it. Jerry had lost his life to the sun's ultraviolet rays. What about an antidote to that? I decided to make sun umbrellas and sun hats. My mission was to protect women fashionably, so they might avoid meeting the same fate as Jerry.

Not knowing anything about the path on which I was

to embark, I spent three years researching importing/exporting, choosing a manufacturer that had a fabric I liked, identifying the colors I wanted, and ordering dye swatches for confirmation. A sample umbrella needed to be found and sent to China for reproduction, and then they would let me know how much fabric was needed for each umbrella and hat.

Some friends expressed doubts that umbrellas and hats were enough, that there needed to be another stylistic component. Ultimately, I decided to design handbags that would coordinate, and in some cases, have a side pocket to hold the umbrella.

Now I was getting into a whole new monetary investment. Living off what I'd inherited from Jerry's death was risky, but I believed there was potential in what I was endeavoring to do. And I could finally combine creativity with commerce. I named my company Soleil Chic.

I began researching handbags by visiting Neiman Marcus and Saks Fifth Avenue, and used those stores as my classrooms. I'd bring a notebook and measuring tape, and sequester myself in the handbag department, making rough drawings of what I saw to give me an idea of what I wanted to do, and how I might combine a feature from one bag and tether it to a feature of another.

I took a marketing class and one in financing at UCLA.

I'd trek downtown to the textile shows at the California Mart and scout out colorful prints for bags. Walking from showroom to showroom to survey these fabrics, an eerie thought crossed my mind: I was entering the world of fabrics, the very thing I had refused to do when my parents had their business. But this time I was doing it on my own without critical voices accosting me at every turn, free to use my creativity and my brain any way I saw fit. I'd select one color from each fabric and then dye my umbrellas that hue so that most of the umbrellas went with the majority of the bags. I was carving out a new career for myself with products I believed were needed and would be desired once women were exposed to them.

My goal was to produce classy products that would be fun and give great protection.

After receiving a list of thirty-five handbag contractors, I found the one I wanted. She contracted for designers who sold bags to Neiman Marcus and Saks Fifth Avenue, the stores for which I wanted to tailor my products.

I definitely found the right person, but when the contractor rattled off questions like: "What kind of connectors do you want?" (*What are connectors?*) and "What kind of feet do you want?" (*feet?*), "Where are you going to go for zippers, and what fabric are you going to use for lining for the bags?" I didn't know the answers to any of these questions.

I asked her to teach me. She said she didn't have the time. But she did it anyway.

The bags were very costly to make, so another big chunk of money went into that. Funds were going out fast and nothing was coming in.

It all came together in March 2004. I delivered my first order of two dozen umbrellas to what was then the Ritz Carlton Hotel in Pasadena, California. Did I make a million dollars? No. Did I feel like I had? Yes, indeed!

Men and sex were secondary at that point. The medication I was on dulled my sexual desires. I had my work, which I threw myself into, I had my dog, and I had my friends. For a while, that was good enough.

I hired a part-time assistant. We decided to take samples and try to sell them to the hotels and boutiques in Palm Springs, two hours outside of Los Angeles, where it was sunny year round. I thought my products would be a natural and easy fit.

In preparation for our first meeting we tested samples. The umbrella I was testing didn't open all the way. My assistant tried one. The same thing occurred. We tested a dozen more. Same result. Panic was rising within me. This couldn't be happening. Prior samples sent from China had tested fine. Why weren't these working?

Finally we found a few that were okay. With trepidation we went to our meetings. In the end nobody bought bags, umbrellas, or hats. When we returned home, I summoned the courage to call some of the people we'd met with to find out the reasons they didn't buy. The answer: Palm Springs was selling sun, not protection from the sun.

But I couldn't give up. I had 2,000 umbrellas, a few dozen bags, and 1,500 hats. From that point on, we had to test every single umbrella before selling any.

Three years of training and thousands of dollars down

the drain. I could have given up right then, and I should have. But I was determined to secure a shipment of umbrellas that worked properly because I believed in the concept: protection from the sun. I knew firsthand what happened when you didn't protect yourself, so I felt compelled to continue.

The umbrellas and hats began to sell, not as easily as the American flag umbrellas, but some sales were trickling in.

I managed to get my umbrellas in *Travel and Leisure Magazine*, and after that the *Today Show* contacted me, requesting that I overnight an umbrella to them. When I saw my umbrella on the *Today Show* I felt like I had really achieved something. Who had I known who had gotten anything on the *Today Show*? Nobody! Following that, after chasing the dream for five years, both my hats and umbrellas were featured in the Travel Section of the *Los Angeles Times*.

For the first time business flooded in. My assistant and I worked from dawn past dusk, packing boxes of umbrellas, hats, and sometimes bags, as orders flashed across my website. We could barely keep up with the demand; the hats and umbrellas sold out.

This dramatic success proved to me that given the right advertising and audience, these products would sell. So I placed another order for 2,000 umbrellas and 1,000 hats. I ordered more handbags as well. There was nothing short of committing an illegal act that I wouldn't have done to get the business off the ground.

The article in the *Los Angeles Times*, as anticipated, ran once. Several weeks later, when it was no longer fresh, sales dropped off. By the time the products were delivered from China four months later, customers had lost interest.

What I needed and didn't have was an advertising budget. And although UV products are substantially more popular now, and have become a staple in fine hotels, cruise ships, and warm weather retail establishments worldwide, sales for Soleil Chic UV umbrellas and hats were at a standstill.

Eventually, I had to fold up the business. My energy, my work, and my passion weren't enough to provide me a livelihood. In trying to become self-sustaining, I had lost a great deal of my inheritance.

WATCH ME – CIRCA 2012

A Short Story

Rod sent me pictures of himself. He was very well endowed and seeing those photos added to my creative flow. This story was conceived with Rod in mind and I sent it to him.

Watch Me

Our good-bye sex was always hot. Whenever my boyfriend, Jake, and I had to be apart, we were propelled into a frenzy of sexual activity. But this time it wasn't the fiery coupling I'd come to expect. After three years together, I wondered if our passion for each other was waning.

Once Jake left on his business trip, I had a choice: stay home and dwell on our lackluster bonding, or go to a girlfriend's party alone. Jake had encouraged me to attend, and my girlfriend promised me she was going to have some new and interesting people, so I threw on a pair of jeans that fit my slim shape well, and a sweater, and headed out.

A party animal at heart, it only took one glass of wine for me to relax. I engaged in conversation with a nice looking man in his early forties. He was very well dressed, and I learned he recently opened an adult store complete with peep show. Having no knowledge of that business, I became quickly intrigued. We conversed for quite a while. He said I had the most stunning head of hair of any woman he'd known. It was long and flaming red. He really liked the way I moved too. My decade as a professional dancer had resulted in a supple body. I liked to think that I was sophisticated but, at twenty-eight I could still be taken in by a compliment. So I lingered longer than I intended.

He mentioned that he had just hired two women to work the peep show but was looking for a third. I was about ready to move on when he offered the job to me! He said that I was a very sensual woman and he thought I'd be a real draw once word got out that I was there. I told him I wasn't interested, that I'd never been to one of those places, and didn't have a good impression of them.

"I've created something different from the ordinary peep show," he assured me, adding that he hoped I would not form an opinion too quickly.

When Jake returned a week later I revealed to him what the man had said, laughing at the ridiculousness of it. But Jake didn't laugh, and in fact suggested I do it, if only for one night. Knowing my outgoing nature, he thought it could be fun for me.

"If you will be my one and only client, I will do it," I said, toying with a piece of hair.

"Won't the owner mind?" Jake asked.

"As long as you pay for my time I don't see why he would object. Besides, he told me the first night's shift would only last a few hours. But maybe this is a bad idea."

"I'll do it," Jake countered.

I was still reluctant, but I called the owner and told him that I'd commit to one night to see how I liked it. He agreed.

I dressed carefully that balmy night, choosing lipstick-red underwear. What there was of it, that Jake had not yet seen. I wore a long, lightweight coat over my lingerie and five-inch-high strappy sandals.

When I entered the adult store I was surprised to find it immaculately clean. It was nicely furnished in beiges and browns. The walls were covered in grasscloth and the dimmed lights gave it a seductive, inviting quality. The owner escorted me to a dressing room, and showed me a locker where I could store my belongings.

Jake, an in-demand architect, planned to meet me after work.

I entered "my room," as the owner called it. A beautiful high-backed chair awaited me, which I settled into comfortably. I didn't expect to see floor-to-ceiling windows. This was not at all what I imagined (small window, decaying atmosphere), but rather expansive, contemporary, and pristine.

I noticed the clock on the wall in front of me. Jake was supposed to have been there by now. Starting to feel apprehensive that a customer might show up and occupy the booth, I had a momentary urge to flee. Just then, out of the corner of my eye, I glimpsed a tall man with a day-old scruff I thought was Jake. I was relieved! He sat down and then, as I took a closer look, I realized my mistake.

The man smiled at me. I smiled back. I worried about where Jake was, but I was stuck. Now my time belonged to this stranger.

In this modern-day peep show, we could communicate easily since telephones had been replaced by microphones, one above me and one above the man. Our hands were totally free.

He directed me to masturbate. I figured that was what I was there for, so I slipped my hand beneath my panties and began circling my clit with my fingers.

"Oh no," he said. "Panties off."

I hesitated a moment, then I did what he asked,

297

exposing my milky white pussy. I resumed touching myself.

"Open your legs wide, please."

I slowly pushed my knees apart with both hands. I saw this in a movie once and thought it was provocative. I was just inches away from the window; he had a clear view of my cunt.

"Nice," he said.

For a limited time, this particular store offered customers a substantial discount if they allowed themselves to be filmed. I had expressed interest in advance, thinking it would be something Jake and I could share later. When I saw the red light blinking I realized this stranger, not Jake, would take the role of leading man. It took me a moment to feel okay with it, but I concluded Jake would want to know what happened and now he could see for himself. And I knew he got turned on by watching.

The man's hand slid down between his legs. He started stroking himself and moaned a little as he observed me. I could see he was enjoying the show. He was still fully dressed, but what he was doing was turning me on.

He unzipped his trousers and pulled out his stiff cock. I began a licking motion with my tongue using my finger as a substitute dick and he became even more excited. My clit had become so hard; I wished there wasn't a window between us. His penis wasn't as big as Jake's but it was big enough. I tried to hold back but I was so aroused I couldn't stop myself; my explosive release completely took the man over the edge and he unloaded huge streams of cum. We were both very expressive; he grunted loudly and I cried out. After a few moments, he pulled up his slacks, and as he put himself together he nodded and left the booth. An attendant did a quick cleaning and then Jake arrived.

I told Jake what happened and he asked me to masturbate again so he could watch and revel in the same thing. I parted my legs and began rubbing my clit. As Jake watched me masturbate, just like the other man, he unzipped his jeans and wasted no time stroking himself. I looked at him and smiled. I knew I was giving him a good time.

"I'm going crazy watching you, baby," he said. "Knowing I can't have you right now. I'm going to cum soon."

"No baby, don't cum yet," I responded. "It'll be better if you can wait."

I pretended I was licking his cock, like I had done earlier with my customer.

Jake moaned, reaching a whole new level of arousal, as I knew he would.

"This is going to be so good for you," I reassured him.

I parted my thighs wider, completely opening up myself to him. I paused for a moment just to catch my breath and so Jake could catch his, then I continued enjoying my own touch and smiled as he stroked himself faster.

"I need to cum, baby," Jake pleaded.

"Okay, but it has to be a real good one. I want you to squirt all of it at me, will you do that?"

"Oh yes baby, I will, I promise."

Jake let go and had the most intense orgasm I had ever seen him experience, and I climaxed also. And what a climax it was! It must have lasted a full minute and I felt it course through my entire body.

After we finished and gathered up our belongings, Jake and I met back at home, and as we watched the DVD of the other man and me, he gave me a powerful fucking, one that lasted, on and off, throughout the night.

In the morning, after seeing what it did for our libidos, we decided I shouldn't take the job but that we would create our own peep show, occasionally inviting a stranger home with us to watch me. We'd film it, of course. And just knowing we were going to embark on this adventure sent us into another heart-thumping round of through-the-roof sex.

Alex Again – 2013

Alex emailed me that he was back in the states and wanted to come see me. I was reluctant after the last time, but finally we agreed on a date.

He called me the morning he was to see me. He was in Los Angeles. This was actually going to happen. I was about to meet Alex.

I told him I would meet him downstairs. I didn't want him to see the interior of my low-cost housing until we connected in person. I stood outside by the entrance. A short Japanese man came rushing toward me. For an instant, I thought, *Oh God, is that* him?

Then a tall man came into view, whose face I recognized as the one I'd seen in the emails. Alex. Fresh from Maine (he was only in Virginia temporarily), had finally arrived. He brought me a camel hair blanket back from Afghanistan. Sweet. I liked him!

We went out for a cup of coffee to become acquainted.

Afterward, I suggested a movie. I was attracted to him, but was at a loss as to how we should spend our visit together. I couldn't just have sex with him. I needed time.

We decided to go the movies and saw *The Hurt Locker*. That was the perfect film to see together. Some of it was meant to take place in Afghanistan. Alex said later that it had been very realistic.

I had asked Alex to make a reservation at a hotel, so if either of us felt uncomfortable he would have a place to stay. If not, we could enjoy being away together.

We checked into the Hyatt Regency in Long Beach later that day and were shown to a very nice room overlooking the water. We had some drinks and hung out for a while in the room, making small talk. He was not pushy, which I appreciated. When we got hungry, we went downstairs and had dinner at the upscale restaurant in the hotel.

When we returned to the room, we kissed. I enjoyed it and hoped this would lead to memorable sex. He undressed me slowly and we made our way to the bed. But Alex couldn't get hard. This was beginning to be a bad habit with the men I was dating. Lisa said a lot of men in their fifties have this problem. Or was it just the ones who had sex with me?

The next day we drove down to the Newport coast, where we had Cucumber Mist Martinis and lunch right on the beach at the Beachcomber Café at Crystal Cove. I had been there before and loved it. It's kind of old-fashioned, with floors made of wooden slats and music from the thirties and forties. It was easy to feel you were on a vacation there. We spent a leisurely couple of hours, then returned to our hotel.

We had sex again. This time our bodies intermingled, but our souls never touched. It was not a love connection, not even a sexual connection. Although he had an orgasm inside me, I never felt him.

During the two days we spent together, I constantly stretched to find some common ground with Alex, but his whole life had revolved around fixing military planes. He was a man who lacked either the time, or interest, to develop himself culturally. My interests were reading, writing, films, travel. He had done little of that.

"I'm glad I came out here," he said on the day he left. "Next time I come we'll go back to the Beachcomber." He told me he would call me when he returned to Maine that night.

Alex did call me that night. But his cell phone kept shutting down, so we weren't able to complete our conversation. He sent me an email that he would call when he got his phone fixed. He never did. It was probably just as well.

He did write me several times after he returned to Afghanistan. But I realized we really lived in two different worlds—and then, of course, there was the sex. Without satisfying sex, I wasn't interested in seeing him again.

We exchanged emails for a few months and then we stopped. I was curious to know how he was doing, and every time I heard of civilians being killed over there, I wondered if he was all right, but I knew it was best to leave it alone.

He Could Practically Be My Grandson! – 2014

He was only forty! I turned him down innumerable times because of the enormous age difference, but he kept pushing and pressing, determined for me to agree to meet him. I didn't know until the last minute whether or not I would. I kept thinking that upon seeing me, despite my attractiveness, he would make some excuse to leave. Why subject myself to that? The last time I went out with someone in his forties was when I was in my thirties.

~

We walked toward the entrance of the restaurant, El Torito, of course, from different directions at the same time.

"Lynn?"

I nodded.

"Patrick?"

He smiled. "Hungry?" he asked.

"Yes," I said.

"Let's get lunch."

And with that, I knew he was attracted to me. I got a rush from it, I admit it.

I didn't remember the maître 'd from prior visits, and I didn't know if he remembered me, but I wouldn't have been surprised if he had because he ushered us to a secluded area of the restaurant out of view of other diners. No one would have to watch my romantic antics were there going to be any!

He ordered margaritas, and told me I looked better than my picture, and that he thought I was beautiful. I told him I liked his mouth. He returned the compliment. We enjoyed our drinks and smiled at each other a lot. We were only halfway through them when he made a pronouncement.

"I'd like to be somewhere private with you."

I thought the booth we were in was pretty private.

"Like where?" I asked.

"Like my car."

"Oh," I said, considering the possibility. I had limited time and I told him so. I had signed up for a class in social media.

When I mentioned that I was full, he said, "You can take the rest home."

I smiled, understanding his intention. He wanted to get

to the car.

"Okay," I said.

He paid the bill and we weren't inside his car for thirty seconds before we started kissing each other. I thought Larry was the best kisser I ever had, but this man's kissing put Larry to shame. His mouth enveloped mine. It was the kind of passion I'd been wanting for so long. He took possession of me.

He suggested we go back to my apartment, but I wasn't ready to do that, and I had that meeting to go to. He pulled the car out of the parking lot and drove down a street where there weren't any cars. We began kissing madly again. I couldn't get enough of him. I imagined how his mouth would feel on the nether regions of my body. His hands were everywhere, but it wasn't just the placement of his hands; it was the way he pulled me toward him, with great intensity and passion. Like a man on fire.

He asked me many times if we could go to my place. I said I had to go. We were both so worked up and I felt either we should go to my apartment, or take leave of each other. As much as I enjoyed him, I just wasn't ready to take him home, even if I had no meeting.

∼

I could barely concentrate in the social media class, reliving those incredible kisses of a half hour before, and the way he pulled me toward him as if his life depended on it.

We emailed each other later. He told me he wanted to see me again soon, and he wanted to know if I still thought he was too young. I told him he definitely wasn't too young in the area of passion.

"Our time together was so sexy," he wrote. "Our chemistry is too hot. Thinking of our next meeting is making me hard. I want to be inside you. I want to feel you. I want to make you cum in my mouth. Please let me. Please let me taste you. I'm not looking for lunches with you. I want to spend our time together in private. Please meet me and play with me. I want you. Please give me everything. I want to give you everything. I'm begging. I want to give it to you however you want it. I want to be your fantasy."

Could I let him? Should I let him?

Finale – 2014

So how does my new openness toward sex conflate
with abuse in my childhood? What have I gained by it, and
how will it help me in my life?

I am finding men are more attracted to me in real life,
and that I have a natural ease with myself and my body that
I didn't have before. I'm working out regularly at the gym,
which I haven't done since my early thirties, and I believe
my mind is integrated with my body instead of one fighting
the other. Now that sexual freedom has spilled over into
emotional freedom, I am better able to express myself in
and out of the bedroom. To put it simply, while I have not
met my special man yet, I am definitely enjoying the ride!

As I was writing this, I learned many things. Here are
some of them:

I learned that people can care for you without
expecting blind devotion in return.

I learned that there are some people you can trust with

your feelings, and that those people will trust you back.

I learned that sex can be fun, and that orgasms, in addition to feeling good, make me feel alive and vital, feminine and present.

But most of all, I learned that blaming myself for falling short of expectations, especially my own, is not warranted or deserved, nor is it a requirement for love.

The dark days of my past are now behind me. I'm now open to a new kind of relationship. While I want to be my best for someone, I no longer feel I have to prove myself as a worthwhile person.

As for my parents: I spent my life trying to earn their love and that effort failed miserably. Did I ever love them? Of course I did. But as the years went by, they killed off that love, threat by threat, lie by lie, betrayal by betrayal. The incidences of abuse in this memoir were just a smattering, as they are too numerous to mention in one book. One friend asked me why I thought they did the things they did. My guess is that they needed a scapegoat for their problems, and I was it. Beyond that, I have no idea.

I have not been on any sex sites for over a year and have no plans to return. I view my experiences with them as a transitional phase that served its purpose. But if I feel the need or desire at some point, I have no compunction about signing up again.

While looking for my mate, both soul and sexual, I still have very erotic phone sex with Hank. We engage in down-and-dirty chats that always bring him to climax, and sometimes I have one too.

At seventy-one, I am having spectacular orgasms, long lasting and very powerful, unlike anything I've ever experienced before. True, I am having them by myself, by my own hand. But still, I'm having them, and it's a glorious thing. Hopefully, they'll be with a man someday soon.

I hope that this book has created in you a desire to find your own satisfaction in whatever way you can—real, fantasy, or both. And that you enjoy whatever you choose more than ever before.

And now, the best part: I've told the truth. It's something I have wanted to do all my life.

ACKNOWLEDGMENTS

Special thanks to Carol Gaskin, Editorial Alchemy for her generous contribution to this book on an earlier draft.

Deep gratitude to Christopher J. Lynch, www.christopherjlynch.com for his robust encouragement, steadfast support, and invaluable input.

An appreciation to the Writer's Circle for giving me insightful feedback on early versions of this book, and for the many suggestions that have expanded and enhanced my life as a writer.

Big thanks to Lisa Granger for being my cover model.

Endless love for Lilly Grace whose unflinching belief in my creative talents has spanned decades.